From Trial To Triumph

One Foster Parent's Journey

Betty Daigle Hastings

Table of Contents

My Story 1

History of Foster Care.. 9

The Need for Foster Homes in Your Community 17

So, You Want to Become a Foster Parent?................................. 21

Couples Who Foster.. 25

Advocating for the Child in Your Home.................................. 29

Allegations—They Come With the Territory............................... 35

Allegations—What Can I Do? 41

Lying Behavior... 47

Lying Behavior—Part II 53

Lying Behavior—Part III 57

Stealing Behavior.. 61

Stealing Behavior—Part II.. 65

Fostering Teens—I Can Handle It 73

Fostering Teens—Guidelines... 77

Working With Birth Parents... 83

Working With Birth Parents—Part II..................................... 87

Discipline and Foster Children 91

Foster Children and Sexual Abuse Issues 95

Saving Discouraged Foster Parents 99

Fostering Has Its Rewards 105

My Personal Letter to Foster Parents................................... 109

This book is dedicated first to God for His divine help throughout my life in helping me to understand the reasons for the valleys I went through, the mountaintops I experienced and the power of His saving grace in my life.

Also to Brian Arnold, from Branson, Missouri—a music evangelist and one-handed piano player, gospel singer and songwriter who has not only been a prayer partner but a good friend who gave me the privilege of operating his ministry office. It was through Brian's encouragement and insistence that I was motivated to write this book.

I thank God for each foster parent whose path I have crossed over the years in my teaching, for each opportunity given to bring my experiences and laughter to them and for the opportunity to lighten the load of what they encounter daily in their fostering lives. This book is also for each child who passed through my door in foster care.

To my children, Eddie Daigle, Tamela Daigle White and LeAnn Daigle Dunlap—Thank you for having patience with my frequent travels and for understanding and sharing with me the trials and victories in foster care over the past years.

Born in a small country town
In Brownsville, Tennessee
What the future held for me
Only God in Heaven could see.

Dad left our home, went away to work
So he promised and said
But he left his family to starve
With my mom on her death bed.

A short time later, God called my mom
To her heavenly home
Leaving my brother and me
Fearful, terrified, alone.

An older sister with five kids
Not the right place for us to go
We became wards of the court
Now they ran the show.

We were shipped out of state
Into foster care
Separated, my brother and me
Alone, unloved and scared.

I became an angry teenager
Like so many others today
Didn't understand the reason
We were treated that way.

Five different homes and left each time
Feeling lost and defeated.
No one cared, no love shown
Each time I felt so mistreated,

But now I know that God did not leave
Nor did He ever forsake me,
His watchful, attentive eye was ever present
Only later did I see

My foster care trials were just a part
Of His future plan
My life's mission is to help others
In any way I can.

My Story

"Never do I want anything to do with foster care!" This is what I grew up feeling, not realizing what the future held for me. Today, my entire life is committed to improving the foster care system for children who are forced to grow up being raised by a variety of parents in homes that are unfamiliar to them.

I was born in a small rural area in Haywood County, Tennessee. My dad worked for hire for other area farmers in our small country town. I was the middle child, with an older sister and a younger brother. I love my dad dearly, and as soon as I was old enough to follow him, I became his constant companion, working with him and going places with him any time I could.

Needless to say, at age 13, I was completely heartbroken when dad told us that he was leaving go to work in another state. His promise to me that day is still with me. He said, "Betty, I'm going to have to go find a job out of this small town, but I promise to come back and get you and the rest of the family just as soon as I find a job and a place for us all to live."

That was the last time I saw my dad until after my mom passed away. I can remember from a very early age that my mother was sick most of the time. I did not know what was wrong with her, but I knew that after dad left, she got worse and didn't get out of the house much anymore.

One evening, my brother and I came in from a movie and found mom unresponsive when I called her name. I tried desperately to wake her up from what I thought was sleep. Finally realizing that something was horribly wrong, I called a neighbor for help. It didn't take long for the neighbor to tell me, "Betty, your mother is unconscious, and we need to call for an ambulance." She was taken to the hospital that evening where she lived for one week. I stayed at her bedside during that entire week, but she did not regain consciousness except for one time, and that was the night before she died.

My older sister was married with four small children and expecting her fifth. Her husband had an extreme drinking problem and a very violent temper. They came to the hospital the night before my mom died, and as I sat next to my mom's bedside, my brother-in-law informed me, "You are not to go to your home in the morning. You are to go to our house. Your sister will pick you up."

I did not think much about it, but this was the only time that my mom was conscious. She heard the demanding instructions he had given me. As he left the hospital, my mom remarked to me, "Betty, you can't rest at your sister's house with the four kids, so when Beth {my aunt} comes to the hospital in the morning, let her take you home." Little did I know that these would be the last words that my mom would ever speak to me. No one told me that the doctor had said she probably would not live throughout the night.

So began a nightmare journey of a then innocent 15 year old, a nightmare that would change and affect me for the rest of my life.

When my aunt arrived the next morning, she carried me to my home as my mom had instructed. But as soon as I got home, my brother-in-law drove up and was furious that I had not obeyed him. He beat me viciously with his belt. Sometimes, although I try not think about it, I can still feel his foot in my sides, his fists in my face. His beatings became a nightmare that I would relive over and over.

I was carried against my will to my sister's home and was not allowed to return to the hospital that evening. Around midnight, we got the call. "Get to the hospital as soon as you can. Your mother is dying." Unaware of the seriousness of her condition, I was shocked. We hurried to the hospital, but it was too late. "She's gone," we were told. Sad, bruised and afraid, I bowed my head and cried.

As I stood at the side of my mother's casket in the funeral home, the results of the brutal beating I had received had left multiple bruises on my face, neck, arms and back. The black whelps were clearly visible to everyone present. Someone, obviously upset and concerned by what they saw, made a report to social services.

When the department's social worker came to the funeral home, she examined my bruises and questioned me about what had happened. Appalled by the extent of my injuries, she said, "Due to what has happened to you, we feel that it's best that you and your brother not stay in the home with your sister and brother-in-law."

This was my family, and I was going to be moved. I was going to be sent somewhere to live with strangers! I didn't want to go. I didn't want to leave my friends, my school, my boyfriend. It didn't seem fair. I had just been selected to play on the first string basketball team. I cried. I begged not to be sent away. I didn't feel I had done anything wrong. Why did I have to go? But my tears and pleas to let me stay didn't work. I didn't fully understand what was happening, but I knew that my life was never going to be the same.

At that moment, I wanted to die.

I know the worker was trying to comfort me when she said, "We tried to find someone here in your home town to keep you and your brother, but no one has offered to take you. We have no other choice but to send you to relatives in Baton Rouge, Louisiana." But I was petrified.

My brother and I were picked up that afternoon and placed on a bus bound for our new lives. This was my introduction to the scary world of foster care. We were to be placed in the foster care system in what would be known today as kinship care.

I will always remember that 500-mile bus ride to a strange city, Strangers met us at the bus station, and we were introduced just days after our mother's death to a strange, new word—"foster care." Our new home was made with distant relatives that we had never met. We had never been outside of our home county. As we got off the bus, horrified and scared, we were met by two ladies—an older lady and her daughter. The only good thing was that my brother and I were together. At least I had him to take away some of the loneliness and pain of being separated from the rest of my family.

What happened next was just another nightmare that has happened to so many siblings as they go into foster care.

When we arrived at our destination—our new home—I felt like we were looked over like animals coming into the slaughter house. The daughter remarked to her mom, "Mom, since we already have two boys, we'll take the girl, and you take the boy."

Hurt, confused and feeling great loss already, I had to endure being separated from my 13-year-old brother. It all seemed so unfair. Why did this happen to me? I was angry, hurt and just plain furious at the world!

So many times over the past years, as I've fostered children experiencing that same fear, I have remembered my feelings on that day—the desperation, the uncertainty and the fear caused by not knowing what was next.

The home into which I was placed was a very prominent home in the community. For the short time I was there, I lived the life of a princess with the promise of what was to be a bright, wonderful future. The couple had decided to adopt me. I couldn't believe it was happening to me. It didn't seem real. I began to feel positive again, although I missed my brother.

He had not done so well in his new home. He was so disturbed and unhappy that he was soon sent back to Tennessee to live with other relatives. I didn't want to go. I'd been in my new home for about a year and felt that everything was going to be so much better for me. I was going to be adopted.

But this soon proved to be just another of my fantasies. As we were returning home from the attorney's office one afternoon, I was informed that my dad had been found and would not relinquish his parental rights. The only recourse was to pursue court proceedings. I was both anxious and nervous on the way home. When the adoption procedure was explained to me, I quickly asked the question, "Will I be able to have contact with my brother after the adoption?"

A dead silence fell over the car. I knew something was not right. I knew I had said something wrong. I loved my brother. Even though he had been sent back to Tennessee, I felt close to him. After the losses I had experienced, I could not lose him, too.

When I came home from school the following week, I noticed that my clothes were packed in suitcases and sitting on the front porch. "What's going on?" I said.

"If you cannot let go of your past, then you can have no part in the life of this family," was the response.

I couldn't believe my ears. They fully expected me to forget about my brother whom I had loved so dearly for 15 years.

This memory has been very vivid to me as I've worked with sibling groups over the past years. When I see new groups of siblings come into foster care, I always think back and remember the bonds that tie families together. Those bonds should receive the utmost consideration in the adoption process.

My next placement was even more traumatic and the move more devastating. Early one morning, my foster mom was at the hospital with one of her biological children. While she was gone, her husband decided to make sexual advances toward the lonely 16-year-old girl living in his home. Because I resisted his advances and ran from him, I found my bags packed once again and waiting for me when I returned from school. Another quick move to a strange placement followed. To this day, I do not know what this foster mom was told, nor was I ever given an opportunity to express my side of what had occurred to anyone. The story of her husband's advances stayed my secret. After all, who would listen to a foster child who had already been taken from two foster homes? Once again, I felt alone, unhappy and angry. All I wanted was for someone to show me a little love and attention.

It became harder for me to adjust after this incident, but over the years, the experience taught me to have an open mind, to listen to foster children as they come into my home with understanding that they are hurting and need someone to believe in them. This certainly was a chapter in my life that has been instrumental in working with children that have been sexual abused.

During all of my placements, I endured all sorts of atrocities, but I was able to work part time to pay for my room and board at my last placement. And when I graduated from Baton Rouge High School, I knew my mom would have been so proud of me.

After graduation, I married my high school sweetheart, George Daigle, and we returned to Tennessee. George felt the call to become a minister, and spent the next ten years serving God and the congregations of several churches. We had three children together—Eddie, Tammy and LeAnn. For a while, life was good, and as I built my family, the images of my own childhood began receding, but were never forgotten. Eddie was eight, Tammy was five and LeAnn was three when George succumbed to cancer and died after only ten years of marriage.

Being a pastor's wife for even a short period, I think, was God's way of preparing me for what He had in store for my life. At this point, foster care was no longer in my vocabulary. I simply wanted to forget. I certainly did not think I would encounter anything to do with dealing with children in foster care.

Left alone with three small children for whom I had to provide, I enrolled in a secretarial course. After graduation, I found employment at the court house in Paris, Tennessee, working for the county judge. I was so proud to have that position, although I was shocked to learn that the county judge was also the juvenile judge. I had no idea then how this would affect my life.

It had been about eight years since the death of George when I met and married a wonderful man, Charles Hastings. After much of my life spent struggling to survive and then struggling to care for my children, I thought my life had turned around. I thought I would be able to devote my life to my new husband, my children and my stepson and that I would be very satisfied. But, as often happens, things occur that shake up our world when we least expect it.

The memories of my personal experience with foster care were brought back full force when two little boys were left in the judge's office. They needed a home and placement "just for the weekend," the Judge assured me. All foster parents are very familiar with those words and where they can lead.

I was called into the judge's office and asked to please find a home for the two boys—ages six and seven for the weekend. "Betty, I'm sure you'll know someone that will be able to keep them this weekend," the judge said confidently.

At that time, I had only been married for about a month. I called my husband at work and asked, "Honey, do you love me?" Even though he thought it unusual for me to be calling him in the middle of the day and asking that question, he replied, "Yes, I love you."

Then I asked the big question, "Do you love me enough for me to bring two little boys home, just for the weekend?"

He didn't hesitate. "Yes, of course."

Over the years, it got to be that when I would call him and ask him, "Do you love me?" his response would be, "Okay, how many?"

Before my beloved Charles passed away, it got to be that when I asked him if he loved me, he would answer, "No, but bring them on anyway."

This was the beginning of a long history of bringing children who needed emergency placements home with me. Our county did not have an emergency facility, and at that time, the judge was able to direct emergency placements. My home had an open door.

I received a call one afternoon about a fifteen-year-old boy who had been left at the jail by his father who claimed that he would not take him back home.

By this time, I had accepted the position of juvenile officer in addition to the secretarial position. I hurried to the jail and brought the young man back to my office. After talking with him and listening to his story, my heart was touched, and I asked him if he would like to go home with me. Somehow I knew this would not be an emergency placement. I felt this teen needed a possible permanent placement until something could be worked out for him.

After all the emergency placements that had been through our home, this was the first approved placement. Charles and I became approved foster parents for the state. As I'm sure most foster parents have experienced in their fostering, it's hard to say "no" when asked to take a child in need of a placement. Soon we lost count of the children we cared for, as more than 350 children have found temporary placement in our home during our twenty seven years of marriage. From these children, two eventually became our adopted sons. One of these children lived with us for seven years and was adopted the month before Charles died as a result of that dreaded disease, cancer.

Betty Daigle Hastings

My own memories of being a foster child have been an invaluable tool for me throughout the years in my fostering experiences. I know what it feels like to experience loss in so many areas. I know what it's like to be separated from people you love. I know what it's like to have the feeling that no one cares, that no one wants to listen to you. I know what it's like to be angry, hurt, depressed and have low self-esteem. But I also know what a blessing you can receive by opening your home and your heart to a hurting child placed in care.

I thank God every day for giving me an opportunity to work with foster children and that I can use my experience to help reach them, to show them that there is life after foster care. I have been blessed with the ability to have worked with various agencies and served in many related areas of foster care. I spent five years working for the University of Tennessee, training foster parents and state workers. So many wonderful opportunities have come my way as I served as the president of four local county associations, then as state association president for Tennessee for six years. During this time, I also held various positions with the National Foster Parent Association, including the position of chairperson for the Council of State Affiliates and NFPA Conference.

I also enjoy being able to write and present workshops. For my workshops, I draw from my own experiences to discuss topics foster parents face when struggling with issues relating to children placed in their homes. This has been a challenging, yet rewarding passion for me throughout my life.

What I went through has encouraged me to put my experiences, my thoughts and some of my fostering knowledge into the pages of this book. I hope it will benefit everyone who reads it and help them gain a better understanding of how to go about "Overcoming the Trials in Foster Care." My goal is to provide encouragement and information to foster parents who open their homes and hearts to troubled young children and to present a complete picture of every aspect of fostering for those who may not be familiar with the process.

8

History of Foster Care

Foster care has existed in the United States for the past 150 years. In 1636, less than 30 years after the founding of Jamestown Colony, at the age of seven Benjamin Eaton was America's first foster child. Back then, there were no regulations about how these children should be treated, and some were treated little better than slaves.

A more formal foster care program was established in the mid-1800s in an attempt to solve the problems foster children were experiencing. In the early 1900s, evaluations of foster parents began to ensure they were able to adequately care for the children, and the government began paying them for that care. Records were kept, children's individual needs were considered when placements were made and the federal government began supporting state inspections of family foster homes. Services were provided to natural families to enable the child to return home, and foster parents were viewed as part of a professional team working to find permanency for dependent children.

Today, we have a system that provides care and protection, and there are many other programs that ensure safety, protection and a plan for permanency for the child in the future. Emphasis has been placed on keeping families together and ensuring permanency for the child in care. Laws and new regulations have been passed by individual states to ensure that a child does not linger too long in foster care.

Many new foster parents learn, to their dismay, that often public opinion does not view foster homes as the loving, caring partnership system that they are designed to be. Many discouraging and disappointing events have caused good foster homes to close their doors to children in need. Allegations made against foster parents and lack of support and opportunities to speak out as the caretaker of the foster child has led to foster home shortages in many states.

In an attempt to save good homes that offer promise and relief, many states have now adopted through legislation a Foster Parent Bill of Rights. This legislation gives explicit rights to foster parents and clarifies certain responsibilities for foster parents in their often seemingly unappreciated duties to their agency and the children in their care. The legislation further points out the needed partnership between foster parents and the agency. I am proud to say that I was a part of the Tennessee legislation, and Tennessee's law has been used throughout the nation as the model for other states to build their own foster care legislation.

An example of the Tennessee legislation is as indicated in TCA 37-2-415. Foster Parents' Rights reads in part:

(1) The department shall treat the foster parent or parents with dignity, respect, trust and consideration as a primary provider of foster care and a member of the professional team caring for foster children;

(2) The department shall provide the foster parent or parents with a clear explanation and understanding of the role of the department and the role of the members of the child's birth family in a child's foster care;

(3) The foster parent or parents shall be permitted to continue their own family values and routines;

(4) The foster parent or parents shall be provided training and support for the purpose of improving skills in providing daily care and meeting the special needs of the child in foster care;

(5) Prior to the placement of a child in foster care, the department shall inform the foster parent or parents of issues relative to the child that may jeopardize the health and safety of the foster family or alter the manner in which foster care should be administered;

(6) The department shall provide a means by which the foster parent or parents can contact the department twenty-four (24) hours a day, seven (7) days a week for the purpose of receiving departmental assistance;

(7) The department shall provide the foster parent or parents timely, adequate financial reimbursement for the quality and knowledgeable care of a child in foster care, as specified in the plan; provided, that the amount of such financial reimbursement shall, each year, be subject to and restricted by the level of funding specifically allocated for such purpose by the provisions of the general appropriations act;

(8A) The department shall provide clear, written explanation of the plan concerning the placement of a child in the foster parent's home. For emergency placements where time does not allow prior preparation of such explanation, the department shall provide such explanation as it becomes available. This explanation shall include, but is not limited to, all information regarding the child's contact with such child's birth family and cultural heritage, if so outlined;

(8B) During an emergency situation when a child must be placed in home-care due to the absence of parents or custodians, the department of children's services may request that a criminal justice agency perform a federal name-based criminal history record check of each adult residing in the home. The results of such check shall be provided to the department, which shall provide a complete set of each adult resident's fingerprints to the Tennessee bureau of investigation within ten (10) calendar days from the date the name search was conducted. The Tennessee Bureau of Investigation shall either positively identify the fingerprint subject or forward the fingerprints to the Federal Bureau of Investigation within fifteen (15) calendar days from the date the name search was conducted. The child shall be removed from the home immediately if any adult resident fails to provide fingerprints or written permission to perform a federal criminal history check when requested;

(8C) When placement of a child in a home is denied as a result of a name-based criminal history record check of a resident and the resident contests that denial, each such resident shall, within five (5) business days, submit to the Tennessee Bureau of Investigation a complete set of such resident's fingerprints to the Tennessee criminal history record repository for submission to the Federal Bureau of Investigation;

(8D) The Tennessee Bureau of Investigation may charge a reasonable fee, not to exceed seventy dollars ($70), for processing a fingerprint-based criminal history record check pursuant to this subdivision (a)(8);

(8E) As used in this section, "emergency situation" refers to those limited instances when the department of children's services is placing a child in the home of private individuals, including neighbors, friends, or relatives, as a result of a sudden unavailability of the child's primary caregiver;

(9) Prior to placement, the department shall allow the foster parent or parents to review written information concerning the child

and allow the foster parent or parents to assist in determining if such child would be a proper placement for the prospective foster family. For emergency placements where time does not allow prior review of such information, the department shall provide information as it becomes available;

(10) The department shall permit the foster parent or parents to refuse placement within their home, or to request, upon reasonable notice to the department, the removal of a child from their home for good reason, without threat of reprisal, unless otherwise stipulated by contract or policy;

(11) The department shall inform the foster parent or parents of scheduled meetings and staffing, concerning the foster child, and the foster parent or parents shall be permitted to actively participate in the case planning and decision-making process regarding the child in foster care. This may include individual service planning meetings, foster care reviews, and individual educational planning meetings;

(12) The department shall inform a foster parent or parents of decisions made by the courts or the child care agency concerning the child;

(13) The department shall solicit the input of a foster parent or parents concerning the plan of services for the child; this input shall be considered in the department's ongoing development of the plan;

(14) The department shall permit, through written consent, the ability of the foster parent or parents to communicate with professionals who work with the foster child, including any therapists, physicians and teachers who work directly with the child;

(15) The department shall provide all information regarding the child and the child's family background and health history, in a timely manner to the foster parent or parents. The foster parent or parents shall receive additional or necessary information, that is relevant to the care of the child, on an ongoing basis; provided, that confidential information received by the foster parents shall be maintained as such by the foster parents, except as necessary to promote or protect the health and welfare of the child;

(16) The department shall provide timely, written notification of changes in the case plan or termination of the placement and the reasons for the changes or termination of placement to the foster parent or parents, except in the instances of immediate response for child protective services;

(17) The department shall notify the foster parent or parents, in a complete manner, of all court hearings. This notification may include, but is not limited to, notice of the date and time of the court hearing, the name of the judge or hearing officer hearing the case, the location of the hearing, and the court docket number of the case. Such notification shall be made upon the department's receipt of this information, or at the same time that notification is issued to birth parents. The foster parent or parents shall be permitted to attend such hearings at the discretion of the court;

(18) The department shall provide, upon request by the foster parent or parents, information regarding the child's progress after a child leaves foster care. Information provided pursuant to this subsection (a) shall only be provided from information already in possession of the department at the time of the request;

(19) The department shall provide the foster parent or parents the training for obtaining support and information concerning a

better understanding of the rights and responsibilities of the foster parent or parents;

(20) The department shall consider the foster parent or parents as the possible first choice permanent parents for the child, who after being in the foster parent's home for twelve (12) months, becomes free for adoption or a planned permanent living arrangement;

(21) The department shall consider the former foster family as a placement option when a foster child who was formerly placed with the foster parent or parents is to be re-entered into foster care;

(22) The department shall permit the foster parent or parents a period of respite, free from placement of foster children in the family's home with follow-up contacts by the agency occurring a minimum of every two (2) months. The foster parent or parents shall provide reasonable notice, to be determined in the promulgation of rules, to the department for respite;

(23) Child abuse/neglect investigations involving the foster parent or parents shall be investigated pursuant to the department's child protective services policy and procedures. A child protective services case manager from another area shall be assigned investigative responsibility. Removal of a foster child will be conducted pursuant to Tennessee Code Annotated and departmental policy and procedures. The department shall permit an individual selected by the membership of the Tennessee Foster Care Association to be educated concerning the procedures relevant to investigations of alleged abuse and neglect by the department and the rights of the accused foster parent or parents. Upon receiving such training, such individual shall be permitted to serve as advocate for the accused foster parent or parents. Such

advocate shall be permitted to be present at all portions of investigations where the accused foster parent or parents are present, and all communication received by such advocate therein shall be strictly confidential. Nothing contained within this item shall be construed to abrogate the provisions of chapter 1 of this title, regarding procedures for investigations of child abuse and neglect and child sexual abuse by the department of children's services and law enforcement agencies;

(24) Upon request, the department shall provide the foster parent or parents copies of all information relative to their family and services contained in the personal foster home record; and

(25) The department shall advise the foster parent or parents of mediation efforts through publication in departmental policy manuals and the Foster Parent Handbook. The foster parent or parents may file for mediation efforts in response to any violations of the preceding tenets.

The foster care system has come a long way toward improving the lives of persons opening their homes and hearts to foster children. But, it is only through daily involvement and participation, the meeting of all requirements, training and the ability to stand firm that foster parents, who are often the only voice heard for the child, can help to bring about placement success with permanency for a safe future for the child.

Foster care is a constantly changing process. My hope is that improvements for foster parents and children will continue and that unity and partnership within the program will grow stronger for everyone involved as we work toward the goal of providing loving homes for all foster children.

The Need for Foster Homes in Your Community

Become a Star in Someone's Life

We read and hear of the bad things that are going on in our world today—about children who are abused and neglected and about how the rate of juvenile delinquency is increasing. We should be very concerned about our children. They are our future, our leaders of tomorrow.

The Bible tells us in Proverbs 22:6: *"Train up a child in the way he should go and when he is old, he will not depart from it."* But the problem is that many of our children today are not being trained up in the way they should be. So many are being left to go whichever way they choose without any discipline, without the right training or proper supervision. As a result, they are turning to their peers for wrong leadership. They are turning to drugs and alcohol. They are entering adult hood without the benefit of any structure or spiritual direction.

In Colossians 3:20 we find that, *"Children are to obey their parents in all things."* But the problem is there are parents who are not providing an example that children can follow and obey.

Because of this, the state has had to step in and protect abused, neglected and abandoned children. If the horrendous experiences of these children are not acknowledged and worked through, as they get older, these kids will develop more serious problems. Surveys of the prison populations across the country bear witness to this. For children to be productive and have a happy adult life, they need the right structure, proper supervision and the right influences in their home life.

These children are lonely, hurting and confused. Many times, their parents' whereabouts are unknown, and they have to care for themselves. The state steps can provide temporary placement until such time as problems may be remedied and safely is secured. This safe temporary environment has been labeled as a "foster home" in which one or two parents have opened their hearts and homes to meet the need.

There is a great need for good foster homes in our world today. Sometimes situations are created by abuse, neglect or sickness on the part of the parents. Often, it is the child who creates the need for placement outside of the home through getting into trouble and being ordered by a judge into foster care. What a scary thought and experience to be told, "Today you will go into foster care." If you close your eyes for a moment and try to visualize being taken from your home, your family and your friends, you will barely have a glimpse of the feeling for a child of entering a strange home, unsure of what the future holds. This experience can be devastating.

God has made the responsibility to care for children clear in the scripture. Jesus has shown by his own example how important children are in James 1:27 as He instructs us, *"To visit the fatherless and widowed in their affliction."* We cannot turn our backs on our children in their time of need.

Prospective foster parents have many concerns. Common questions include, "How will I ever be able to give a child up?" "How will my family feel?" "How will I continue to discipline my birth children if I am not allowed to spank a foster child?" "What would I have to change about my life?" "Can they attend church with me?"

Everyone will receive a different answer through pre-service training, the relationship of the person with the worker and through God's direction for their lives.

My answer to, "How could I ever give a child up?" After some of the children I've had in my home, I can honestly say that there were times I was glad to give them up!

Everyone does not feel that they want to or can become a foster parent, but there are many other ways that concerned persons can help and be involved. Giving financially to children's homes and supporting those who are foster parents in the community through encouragement and prayer help meet the needs of a hurting child.

Matthew 25: 35-40 tells us in part, *"For I was hungry and you gave me meat; I was thirsty, and you gave me drink: I was a stranger and you took me in, naked, and you clothed me: I was sick and you visited me. I was in prison, and you came unto me. Then shall the righteous answer Him saying, 'Lord, when did we see you hungry, and fed you or thirsty, and gave you drink? When we saw you a stranger, and took you in or naked and clothed you?' And the King shall answer and say unto them, 'Verily I say unto you, Inasmuch as you have done it unto one of the least of these my brethren, you have done it unto me.'"*

The greatest satisfaction received by a foster parent is to see happiness in the eyes of a child that has been wounded in body and mind and providing the opportunity for a safe, loving permanent home.

To me, foster parenting has been a stepping out in faith experience as Hebrew 11:1 states, *"Faith is the substance of things hoped for, the evidence of things not seen."*

Foster parents are the best recruiters for new homes because we've already been there and done that. We're cried with the hurts, we've celebrated with the joys and happiness. The need is great. I hope that we can always look at the smile on the face of a foster child and feel that we have done our job well and that we continue to work toward recruitment of homes in our communities.

In all of my fostering years, I have not always seen evidence of my hard work with a foster child, but I had the faith to believe that we can only plant the seed and let God give the increase. We have to base our faith on the word of God, and His word will lead us through any heartaches and trials we encounter, whether we can see immediate results or not.

So, You Want to Become a Foster Parent?

What is a foster parent? A foster parent is a person who cares for children or youth who are not in their custody, children or youth who have entered the foster care system.

If I were to ask foster parents why they wanted their home to become a foster home, I'm sure I would get various answers.

We often hear of horrible stories of children who are mistreated, abused or hurt in many ways. Yes, we are concerned. We want to help. We want to step in to see what we can do because we feel compassion and sympathy and often even anger.

For some of us, perhaps we have a feeling of loneliness in our lives. Birth children have grown up, but there's still a desire to do something that brings joy and happiness to others. There is space in the home now, empty rooms where the sound and presence of children are missing. Fostering seems to be the answer. It is a way we can share our love for children through showing them that the world is not always a bad place. Through fostering, we can give them a loving home.

Kinship care has become very popular in our nation. This is a tremendous step forward for the child going into care. To be able to remain with relatives or even special friends, pastors, teachers or other familiar persons helps to make the transition from home to foster care less traumatic for the child.

Foster care is temporary, but when parental rights have been terminated and the child is available for adoption, foster parents have the ability to adopt. When a child has been in your home for a period of time, foster parents that would never have considered adoption, adopt. The largest percentage of adoptions is by foster parents. I am one of those lucky foster parents who has been fortunate enough to adopt.

Are there people who become foster parents for financial assistance? How I wish I could say that this never happens, but I'm afraid that I have met some people who were only interested in fostering for the wrong reasons. When this happens, the foster child, who was placed in the hope of having a happy home life, suffers. Hopefully, this problem can be corrected.

The benefits involved with fostering a child should not include financial gain. We can all agree that if the child is sufficiently cared for not even the board reimbursement is enough to provide for all the needs for a child in care.

As you consider sharing your home with a child in need, you should know that there are state requirements, including:

- Age limits
- Criminal background check
- Fingerprints
- Financial report
- Health checks
- Autobiography
- References
- Pre-service training (Hours required vary from state to state)
- Home visits

After fulfilling all of the requirements, graduation is in order. Then the wait begins for that call from the worker with that first placement. You are now a foster parent!

Becoming a foster parent was a mission given to me by God. The road is not always easy, and often I've questioned, "Is it time to quit?"

So many times, I've made the statement, "After this one, I'm through!" I know many others have said the same thing, but fostering is a commitment. It requires dedication and faith. It is a worthy cause to help a child until he/she can either return home or reach permanency. That's what it's all about.

So you want to become a foster parent with your heart filled with love and a desire to help a hurting child? While it can be difficult, it can also be the most rewarding experience of your life. Many times, there is no special recognition or appreciation. It is job that is done from the heart, and that is where you will find your reward. For whatever time you serve, know that you are making a positive difference in the life of a child.

Couples Who Foster

Fostering can take its toll on the marital relationship, and a couple's strong bond as a team is key to providing support and direction to children in their care. Sometimes it seems that foster parents focus on the child's development and ignore their own development as a couple. Foster parents should take the opportunity to assess their own relationship, to identify ways to improve it and further develop fostering as a team.

To bring a new person into the family changes the relationships of the family members. When you add new persons to a family, there are a lot of extra trips to the doctor, to court, to school and on and on. Sharing also becomes an issue—sharing toys, sharing time that was devoted to your own children or even sharing your spouse. Your own children are going to lose some privacy or space in the home, particularly the bathroom, and have to learn to share with the new faces in the home.

There's a new seat at the table, new rules that must be established, and the family wants to do all they can to make the new child comfortable. You may have to express to your own children that there may be times when they may think you don't love them, but stress that you don't love them any less and that this is not going to change your love for them.

Reinforcement to adopted children is especially important. When we adopted our first foster son, our birth daughter would tell him, "You're special, Mom has to keep me, but you're special because you were chosen to be in our home and part of our family."

Bringing children into your home will change everything. Foster children come with a different lifestyle and are used to many different activities that may be unfamiliar to you. People do things differently in their own homes. In some foster homes, teens are allowed to prepare their own meals. In my home, this was unheard of. I prepare three meals a day and we sit down to eat together. We even snack together. That's not to say that the other is not right, it's just that people are different. Your rules must be explained to children coming into the home. Whatever works best for you and your family is what you need to do. Everyone, including spouses, must come to an understanding about how things will be done. A couple's commitment to be united and respectful of each other will model a healthy, positive adult relationship for the child. This positive relationship may contribute to the child's sense of security and trust, as well as their ideas about relationships.

One of my foster children once asked me, "When do you and Pop fight?"

"Fight?" I asked him, "We don't fight."

His response was that his mom and her boyfriend fought all the time. He said his mom would jump up on her boyfriend's back and beat him in the head. He hadn't seen me and Pop do any of that. I explained to him that first of all, with my size at the time, hopping on Pop's back would mean a trip to the floor for both of us, and fighting was not for us.

That does not mean that Charles and I did not have misunderstandings or those deeply intense moments of discussion. It merely means that we promised each other that having disagreements would be kept away from our birth and foster children. Trying to restrain from having arguments in front of our children was something that we always tried hard to do.

Children who come into care bring their bad baggage and hurting pasts with them—the way they were treated, the way their own families did things, things that had happened to them and the way they view the world. Even babies know that they are in a different place. Children come into foster homes bed-wedding, smoking, having poor hygiene, lying, having poor table manners, stealing, flirting, acting out sexually, and with other things that most families are familiar. All of these things could indicate potential problems. You and your spouse will want to discuss all these possibilities and maybe get your worker involved if you feel the need for their involvement.

You want to ask questions of the worker concerning the child before they are placed in your home to see if there are problems or concerns that you might have. You should not wait until placement is made and then have to address it. Have an understanding of your requirement and expectations from placements readily available, and you and your spouse should both agree on what you expect and what you can best handle.

Within the marriage, communication is the thread that ties everything together You must have good communication and support of each other or your marriage in foster care will definitely be damaged. All too often when fostering, we can lose sight of the little things that mean so much to each of us. It is very important that couples communicate positively to each other. Children who come into your home will know if you are a unified team by how you communicate, how you address problems and how well you work together in both times of stress and enjoyment.

One of the best supports that foster parents have is each other. Foster care is a lot of work, stress and worry, but it can be very rewarding. The emotional roller coaster ride of fostering can either make your relationship stronger or destroy it.

Let's look at the negative side. To destroy a perfectly good marriage with foster care, you could:

- Neglect your marriage by allowing foster care to become your whole world and never making time for one another. You may feel that fostering is your life, but share it. Foster together.
- Allow the child to manipulate through playing you against your spouse. This can get out of hand very quickly. Have a clear understanding about how things will be handled, including decision making, discipline, tasks assigned, etc.
- Argue in front of the kids so they will know you are stressed out and wearing down. All couples have those moments of intense discussion, but if it's within the earshot of children that have been traumatized before coming to your home, you're adding to the existing problem.
- Ignore your own needs by never taking time out for yourself. This

should make you good and cranky. Never enjoy a hobby; take a walk or take time for a bubble bath.

- Take the children's problems personally, and then take your stress and frustration out on your spouse and family. Okay, you've had a bad day. Johnny threw a temper tantrum and threw a book at you. Or birth mom called and cancelled the visit today, Johnny is upset and you're on edge because he's upset. It just gets you so angry so you show your temper, too. Remember to keep your priorities in order and learn to relax.
- Argue with your spouse over the kids. By showing them there is division, you will help to have the children play dad against mom in the future. Keep your arguments away from the kids.
- Don't seek help. When you see problems, don't seek professional help or your pastor for some solutions. Just sweep under the rug and plan to handle by yourself. Refuse to talk about problems or about things that bother you with your spouse. Just explode. Seek resolution as soon as possible and remember everyone encounters problems in fostering and there's nothing wrong with asking for help.
- Don't ever have fun. Foster parents need to have fun and entertainment within their lives. We all need to escape and get away, to have time away from the service of the foster child. This will help you avoid future frustrations.

Foster couples have to examine their life together. They need to nurture their relationship, to make time for each other. If couples learn to take care of themselves, they will be more prepared and have more energy for their children. They will feel more confident and creative even when children spring surprises on them. Foster parents can teach by example.

Fostering can affect a marriage, and parents should be aware of this and strive to always work effectively together teaching children that they are united in decisions and in their role as foster parents. It will make for a much happier home while modeling a good relationship for the kids.

Advocating for the Child in Your Home

Merriam Webster's Collegiate Dictionary defines advocacy as, "the act or process of advocating or supporting a cause or proposal." Many of us believe that advocacy, or speaking up for others, is a critical part of making positive change in our world. It's an education and awareness process. It's a matter of listening, talking with others to identify issues and gathering information. Being an advocate isn't hard; it simply requires commitment, enthusiasm and time involved. Therefore, the definition intended here is the act or process of pleading in favor or supporting a cause. Our cause is for our foster children.

A foster parent is an advocate, a backer, a promoter, a believer, an activist, a campaigner, a fighter and definitely a sponsor who supports an idea or way of bettering the life of a foster child and helping the child to reach permanency.

Advocacy involves helping an individual or a group by offering information and support. Sometimes it means speaking on behalf of an individual or group who are unable for whatever reason to speak for themselves. Advocates represent their view as if they were their own. In the foster care system, children in care certainly fit into this category. Foster parents need to speak up for them and keep in mind that we act in what is in the best interest of children in care. Far too long, foster parents have been the silent group and have let others speak out for them, often without their best interest at heart. Or, at times, there has been no one to speak out at all. It's time for a partnership between foster parents and agencies willing to work together for the best interest of all concerned, especially for our children in care.

I have never seen a time that foster parents are hurting or needing services more than right now. These parents are in need of advocacy or someone to support their cause. It's like looking at a sink full of dirty dishes and hoping that they will get clean. If you sit and wait for someone else to do the dishes, hoping that they will clean themselves, you will soon realize that you must do the job yourself. Advocating and helping foster parents and children in care requires involvement. You can help to get the job done or resolve to face a lifetime of disappointment.

Years ago, foster parents were perceived as being just glorified babysitters. A child was brought into a foster home, without any knowledge of what the future held. Today, many states have realized the importance of support and input of foster parents and what it means to have their support and input in the system.

Before you can advocate in any situation, you must first identify the need, the problem and the issue. We have to keep in mind that there is difference between a symptom and a core problem. For example, for a headache, fever or congestion we may go to the doctor, but the doctor will want to find what is causing these symptoms. Symptoms are just warning signs of a problem that exists. There are times when we can begin working on the symptoms before we actually know what the core problem is or why it exists.

There are six steps for effective self-advocacy that I hope will show you how important you are, what you can do to advocate for the child in your home and how you can apply these steps in your fostering life.

1. Know your rights and where to go to educate yourself about those rights. Some states now have websites, and foster parents can go online to look at their policies and recent changes that may affect their lives. When websites are not available, there are other avenues to be able to keep up with changes. Policies within the system change often, and you can access those policies through

training, day-to-day dealings with your worker or through associations. State and local associations are the best informative,
educational and communication methods that we as foster parents
have.

Another way to know your rights is to obtain a copy and use the
state's Foster Parent Bill of Rights, if applicable. You need to learn
what your rights are and demand that they are carried out as specified by the law. Many states have adopted a bill of rights. If your
state does not have this law and you are interested, you can contact
the National Foster Parent Association for steps to start the process to get one.

2. Define your goals: What goals should foster parents be striving to
   obtain, and where do you start? My advice is to start where you
   see that there is the greatest need.

3. Understand the chain of command and the process of the agency that you're working with. Walk the chain of command. If you
   have a problem with a worker, make contact with them and if that
   doesn't help resolve the problem, ask to speak with a supervisor.
   Travel up that chain of command.

4. Ask for support from others who can answer your questions, including your worker, your local or state association or even from
   a national agency, such as the National Foster Parent Association,
   (NFPA) or the North American Council on Adoptable Children
   (NACAC). You can also get support from other seasoned foster
   parents who have probably experienced some of the same problems you are experiencing.

5. Document everything. I always advise foster parents to keep
   a daily journal about the child in your home. Get in the habit
   of writing down a few comments each day. I would record
   specific events, the positive, the negative, the ordinary and the

extraordinary events. This way, when meetings are held or you meet with the worker, you have specifics that will be helpful when sharing the needs or celebrations of the child.

6. Attend any and all meetings. Foster parents have the right to be heard, especially in court, unless otherwise ordered not to attend by the judge. You can't have a voice if you are not present. If you can't attend a meeting, take the time to write down your thoughts and produce your notes to the person in charge of the meeting.

An important arena for advocating for your foster child, yourself and other foster parents lies with your relationships with your state and federal legislators. If you want the input and power to help change policies, work on the relationships with your government representatives.

You must also be an advocate for the foster child within the education system. It's a proved fact that foster children have the poorest grades, largest absentee rate and the largest drop-out rate. There is a great need for advocates to help foster children receive a proper education.

By learning advocacy skills, you can improve your ability to influence people and increase the awareness of care-giving issues. Always keep a child-centered approach with the child's best interest at the top. You will feel a feeling of great accomplishment when you see the needs of foster children being addressed through your efforts.

A group of men were fishing off the shore of a river. One of the men noticed a child floating downstream. He immediately jumped into the water and brought the child to safety.

Before long there was another child seen floating down the river. His fishing partner jumped in for the child out and saved his life. After about four more of such incidents, the men were really becoming alarmed. One of the fishermen left the group and headed upstream.

"Wait!" they called out. "We need you to stay and help us. Where are you going?"

The man quickly replied. "I'm going up stream to see who is throwing these children in the water, endangering their lives and see what I can do to correct this at the core of the problem."

Foster parents may not have to wade in water to save children, but we have to get involved. We have to provide support and do what we can to advocate for the children in our homes.

Not being educated in advocating and having a horrible fear of not knowing what to do to help a child with extreme problems resulted in a child being removed from my home once. That was the last resort after examining all resources and searching for help. Sadly, there are times we are forced to understand that some children's problems are beyond what we are able to handle.

Hurting Hearts

On that day in February a baby left on the doorstep,
a late cold evening in the rain,
Wrapped in a blanket, with just a torn tee shirt,
the reason, we could not explain,
It didn't take long to know he was desperately in need
of love and special care, too,
Offering our home for love and security, what the future held,
we didn't have a clue,
With days and years passing, the problems multiplying,
it was so hard to understand,
All resources and crisis intervention used
and to finally explore another plan,
Foster parents' hearts are broken when they feel that
they've done all that they can
And how it hurts to ask for removal of the child
whose life they felt held in their hand,
But, now they hope for the best to come out of the
painful decision they have made,

Knowing the child is in the hands of God
with a successful future, they prayed.
Having faith that the day will come,
the child remembers something taught in the past,
And one day they will see the results
of their hard work and prayers answered at last.

Such was the situation of a young boy placed in my home with multiple problems. We worked with him for years, but finally we had to realize that we were unable to meet his needs. He left our home through juvenile court with 17 counts of burglary, drugs and threatening my life with a butcher knife. This was a very scary experience. He retuned to visit a few years ago, an adult now. As he stood at my door with his hand behind him, he asked if he could come in. I was a little apprehensive because I was at home alone. But I gave him my approval. He suddenly jerked the hand from behind his back and said to me, "Here, this is for you." In his hand was a single rose and a Mother's Day card. I could not hold back the tears. We never know what impact we make on a young life.

This particular case helped me learn how important it is for foster parents to be willing to step out, to advocate for help, to understand why the child is not receiving the services needed and to work toward a safe environment in a permanent family.

As foster parents, it is imperative that we be the voice for our children in care.

Allegations – They Come with the Territory

My first allegation came after 15 years of fostering. I received a call from the worker stating that my three-year-old foster child, who had just come in from day care, would be picked up by the transporter and brought to the office. It didn't occur to me for a few moments that I had a problem to be concerned about, but all of a sudden it hit me. Something was strange about this. I always carried my foster children to appointments and visitation, so why was he being picked up? I immediately called the worker back and asked what was going on. I was told not to get excited. She said she didn't want to tell me, but I had had an allegation. A what? I don't remember ever being told about anything about an allegation. I couldn't believe it, nor did I understand what was going on. What was an allegation?

My foster son was supposed to have a black bruise from a belt across his buttocks. The worker gave me the length of the mark and told me how low it was supposed to be below the waist line. I knew he did not have any bruise from any belt I had used because I had not hit him. She advised me to just stay calm, to let them pick him up and examine him. She told me again to stay calm. STAY CALM?

We were new to the neighborhood and the community. I was afraid my new neighbors would hear of it and wonder what kind of person had moved into their neighborhood. It was a very terrifying, traumatic experience. My husband was at the prison working, and I could not contact him, which only added to my distress.

I think I aged 15 years during those two long hours. I walked the floor, cried and wondered what my new neighbors would think of me if they heard they had a child beater next door.

The worker finally brought the child back. "Just as we thought," she said. "Not a scratch on him. See, you had nothing to worry about."

I wonder how many foster parents have experienced the same kind of incident and have been told there is nothing to worry about. I realized later that there should be some help for foster parents who have to go through such trauma and worry. I had never heard of any place that offered help, advice or direction as to how to handle such an allegation. The outcome of my traumatic experience was that the day care worker who had made the report had reported the wrong mother to the department.

This experience taught me a very important lesson. Foster parents needed information that helped them deal with this possible eventuality. It was important to me that foster parents realize that allegations come with the territory, so I developed what I hope can give insight to this dreaded fiasco.

One of the most horrible things that can happen in the life of a foster parent is to have that experience of an allegation. Chances are that eventually there will be an allegation, especially for long-term caregivers of multiple children. There are no definite preventions, but there are some possible safeguards to help foster parents avoid an allegation. It helps to know what to expect when one does come and to understand how it can affect their lives.

An allegation is a call or a statement made by someone of an incident declared to be the truth by the person reporting the alleged incident. Keep in mind here that the emphasis is on "declared to be the truth of the alleged incident." Once a report of abuse has been given to an agency, the nightmare begins.

An allegation brings shock, devastation and a feeling of helplessness to the foster family. An allegation of any nature is devastating, and it becomes difficult for the foster family to get back into the mainstream of everyday life. I don't feel we are ever the same after an allegation. While we may be a little disappointed, frustrated, confused and embarrassed, I would hope that we will also become a whole lot wiser and more knowledgeable from the experience.

Who makes allegations?

- Neighbors
- Friends
- Birth Family
- Other foster parents
- Department/agency workers
- School teachers
- Other professionals
- Foster children

The caller's identity is confidential. In some states where foster parents are given the opportunity to view their records, they can read any allegations in the file but will not know who made them.

When foster parents first enter the world of fostering, they are excited, enthusiastic, willing and eager to meet any of the challenges that they feel they might face. They are anxious to get that first foster child, and it never occurs to them that there is such a thing as an allegation. Maybe it was mentioned in the pre-service training, but that was something that happened to others, not to them. Besides, they were going to be so careful and take such good care of the children placed in their home that an allegation would never happen.

Well, let me tell you, you can be the best parent, the most concerned and most conscientious person on this earth and still receive an allegation when you least expect it. I think sometimes that if prospective foster parents knew of the perils inside this often crazy world of caring for abused and neglected children, I wonder if they would pursue the world of fostering.

Are foster parents held to a higher standard than others outside the foster care system? Yes, I think so. Our constitutional rights ensure innocence until proven guilty. But foster parents whom I have had contact with after an allegation do not feel that this is the case. Many in the foster care system feel we are guilty until proven innocent.

We also have to realize that our system has to take a deeper look into allegations and protect the child. The safety of the child is first and foremost.

Let's look at the types of allegations that we may see reported:

- Physical abuse
- Environmental neglect
- Lack of supervision
- Abandonment
- Medical maltreatment
- Substantial risk of sexual abuse
- Substantial risk of physical injury
- Abuse death
- Neglect death
- Drug exposure
- Educational neglect
- Sexual abuse

Every allegation must be investigated and examined. One of the hardest things to remember during this time is that the agency and foster parents should not be at odds during an investigation. A foster parent may want to have an elaborate discussion with the case manager immediately. After all, they may have been fostering for years, been in the agency office almost every day and feel that the worker should know this allegation could not be true. But the worker doesn't respond the way we think they should, and we get this "they think I'm guilty attitude." This causes many feelings of frustration and mistrust on the part of the foster parent.

We have to realize that the case manager has to stay out of it until the investigation is over.

First, a determination has to be made about the seriousness of the incident and if the children in the home need to be removed until the investigation is completed. This decision is based upon the type of allegation, the serious nature of it and the threat to the wellbeing of the foster children in the home.

The goal of an investigation should be to determine what exactly has occurred. If it is determined that the allegation was unfounded, then the process should be to understand why the false allegation was made. These findings could often help to create a workable solution that would keep this from re-occurring in the future. For example, if a child has made the complaint just to get away from the foster home, this needs to be addressed and the worker needs to discuss the action with the child. Should the child be removed in the future, this information should be given to the next foster home.

Investigators work to determine if the allegation is founded or unfounded. If it is determined that the incident is founded, action is taken immediately. If the allegation is unfounded, the foster parents should be notified of the outcome in a timely manner. It is during this time that we lose many good foster parents. Many spend their time as I did, walking the floor and wondering what the future holds, knowing they are not guilty. Understanding agency procedure can certainly help foster parents understand the process. Even though it is hard to wait and wonder, it could be a key to holding on to good parents as they go through the fearful allegation process.

I wish the statement that, "foster parents never abuse the children placed in their home was true," but we know it isn't. It's a fact that there are foster parents who have been found guilty of abuse, which has made an impact on the news media and the community as a whole. One bad apple in the basket seemingly has affected the entire basket and helped to influence the minds of the public about foster parenting.

Regardless if an allegation is founded or unfounded, it has a tremendous impact on the foster family. All too often the foster child's placement in another home may be difficult after an allegation is made. Foster parents are left feeling hurt, discouraged and questioning why or if they should continue fostering. A lot of good homes have been closed due to an unfounded allegation and because foster parents do not understand that allegations come with the territory.

Allegations— What Can I Do?

Foster parents have to remember that the primary focus in an allegation is always the protection of the child. After an allegation is received, it may be at that time the Child Protective Service Worker (CPS) may feel that removal of the child is necessary, but that does not necessarily mean that the child won't be returned at the determination of an unfounded allegation. It's so hard for foster parents to grasp this at the time of removal. However, it also does not mean that the child will be returned at the close of the investigation.

There are some suggestions that might help prevent allegations from occurring. When foster parents are contacted about placement, it helps to ask questions about the child's history. This will help foster parents decide if they can handle the child's problems and gives them insight about what to expect.

It is wise to put safeguards in place before an allegation is made:

- Document everything in a spiral notebook, including:
  Behaviors—changes in a child's normal behavior.
  Talks—what happened, who was there, what was said and why.
  Events of the day—unusual things. Meetings with birth parents.
  Phone calls to and from the child, including date and time.
  Reactions of the child before and after visits.

Any disciplinary action — what happened, what you did, discipline given.

- Keep in touch with your worker on a regular basis, especially if you're experiencing problems with the child. Share the documented materials.
- Always leave doors open when you talk to a child.
- Don't be alone in a room, particularly in a bedroom, with a child when you're having a heart to heart talk. Have a third party present if possible to prevent a distorted version being told to the agency about what happened.
- Don't make stupid threats or ever threaten the child, even if you don't mean to carry it out.
- Be careful about the type of discipline you use. Make sure the punishment fits the offence.
- Don't use verbal ridicule or humiliation. This is very hard to prove, but it's often used against the parent. A foster parent once had a corrective action placed against her because the child stated that the parent called her stupid. The parent said she only told the child, "That was a stupid act you pulled."
- Never deny contact with the birth parents if the worker has approved it. I once talked to a foster parent who stated that if the child got into trouble, she would not let the child talk to her birth mother on the phone. Be certain to discuss any questionable action with your worker.
- Familiarize yourself with policies and rules surrounding Child Protective Services (CPS) issues. States rules and policies vary, so be knowledgeable about what applies in your state.
- Don't be afraid to say no to a requested placement. You don't want to have a problem arise when you know from the beginning that a child should not come into your home.
- Take pictures often, particularly during visits. Be able to show that, yes, mom was there on such and such date and that the child was also present. Share those pictures with the worker.

- Display written house rules so that children can see them and know what to expect while in the home. Make sure every child understand the rules of the home. Also, share these rules with your worker.
- Network with other foster parents. Associations are wonderful places to pass along information. The buddy system is great in an association. We've all heard of the television program "Survivor." I can tell you that foster parents, particularly new foster parents, need to keep in touch with experienced allegation survivors.
- Have open discussions with the child. If you find that a child has reported abuse or made an allegation about a foster parent prior to coming into your home, talk to them about it openly. Tell the child that you plan to protect him/her and yourself.
- Education/Training—Educate yourself about what can happen, what to expect and be knowledgeable about all possibilities. The unknown is to be feared, but education and knowledge will help if you receive an allegation against you.
- Know your limits. If you are not comfortable handling children with certain challenging backgrounds and behaviors don't set yourself up by bringing these children into your home. Make certain your worker is aware or your limitations and that they are documented in your records with the agency. My limits include children with severe medical problems. I think foster parents who foster children with severe disabilities are angels with wings and crowns of gold. I have worked with children with many behavior problems—children who have stolen my car and my jewelry, who have damaged doors and ceilings, as well as other bizarre incidents. I know my limits and won't set myself up for known failure for me or the child.
- Avoid teasing, horseplay, wrestling and suggestive language. These are acts of intimacy, and intimacy is what sexually abused children often resist. The child may get a different message than you intended with this type of close contact.

- Be clear on rules of dress, privacy and touching, and never place yourself at risk by being alone with a child who has been sexually abused. That might cause an allegation for negligence on your part.
- Agree on rules, boundaries, and consequences
- Use common sense and good judgment. An example is a parent leaving her child in the car with the engine running while running into the grocery store. When she returned, a policeman threatened to remove the child. Lack of good judgment could cause you to could lose your license and have your foster children removed.
- Try to stay positive/cooperate. If you know the allegation will be proven false, try not to presume they are just trying to find you guilty. Have patience and try to cooperate.
- As a last resort, hire an attorney. If you feel that things are getting out of hand and not going like they should, get legal assistance.

Allegations are real. Foster parents can never really be prepared for an allegation, and you can't prevent an allegation. But, you can to survive it if you are prepared and safeguard yourself. Know you are not alone. Remember, we must protect our families and ourselves first. Foster parents are survivors, but we don't have to "pull this alone." We can be prepared and take precautions and take advantage of safeguards. There is life in foster care after an allegation.

Questions to Ask Before Taking a Placement

Name: _____

Age: _____   Sex: _____

Reason for being in care: _____

Delinquent Placement: Yes_____   No_____

If so, what is the delinquent behavior? _____

_____

Behavioral issues which may affect the care and supervision the child:

- Acts out sexually
- Aggressive
- Assaulting
- Bedwetting
- Fire Setting
- Habitual Lying
- Runaway
- Smoking
- Stealing
- Substance Abuse

History of Physical or Sexual Abuse: Yes_____   No_____

Describe special medical or psychological needs of the child:
(medicines, etc.)

_____

_____

Check current infectious diseases:

- Chicken Pox
- STD (other than HIV)
- Hepatitis
- Measles
- TB
- Any Other

Lying Behavior

Katie, age 15, was placed in my home for just for the weekend. Foster parents know about these words, "just for the weekend." We were told that she would be with us until arrangements could be made to send her to a home for girls.

I had made plans to go to the North American Council on Adoptable Children (NACAC) conference in North Carolina. We had two foster daughters, so my husband and I decided to have respite for the girls. He would be traveling with me.

Katie was placed with an elderly couple for the respite period. On the second day of the conference as I was walking back to my hotel after a tiring day, my cell phone rang. I thought this was a bit unusual because the worker asked me if I had had a good day. Then she blew my mind with her next statement.

It seemed that Katie was found the evening that she went to the couples' home with a strange smoke smell coming from her bedroom. The couple had called the worker and expressed concern as it did not smell like a normal cigarette odor. The worker had told them if it happened again to call her. They did the very next day. The worker went out to investigate and found Katie with a marijuana cigarette. The worker asked where she had gotten it. Katie stated that she got it from her foster mom, Betty—that Miss Betty gave all of her foster children marijuana to smoke. When asked if she knew where the marijuana was kept in the foster home, Katie responded, "Yes, it is in the ceiling above the tile in my bedroom."

The worker said that they would have to take an officer and the drug dog into my home to do a search. Speechless and traumatized by what she had said, I had a quick response to the false accusation of giving marijuana to my foster children. It really upset me thinking of a dog tearing up my property.

I offered to come home, but the worker didn't think that was necessary. Besides, I knew that before I could get home, it would all be over. Now, I knew that I did not ever give marijuana to any child, birth, foster, or neighbor kids. But, I wondered if Katie said she knew where some was hidden, would they believe that it wasn't mine? I had other teens there before and who knew had been left there.

The search was held, but they did not find anything in the ceiling.

Do foster kids lie? I think any foster parent can successfully answer this question. But I now understand the statement, "Foster kids do not lie." It merely means that anything that a foster child alleges to must be looked into and determined to be a lie or the truth. One uninvestigated allegation could result in a child being hurt or killed.

I bet all of us at some point in our life have told a lie or some type of falsehood. Maybe we've even taken something that wasn't ours. Not a big crime and we weren't punished for it, but it still remains in the back of our mind. None of us are perfect.

When I do my workshop, I use an activity where I ask foster parents to write something about themselves in the past, either when they have told a lie or taken something that they know they shouldn't have. My purpose is to show that we're all guilty of having skeletons in our closets. This helps open our eyes and helps us deal with the problems that our foster children have within their lives.

I have received many comments, unsigned of course, of foster parents confessing to taking chewing gum, taking paper from the office, slipping out windows, being abused by the their parents, raped, and on and on. This simply shows we all make mistakes and have done things that we shouldn't have. It also shows that we have overcome these things.

I often read some of the remarks to the group. One of the most bizarre remark was on a card that I received where the person was currently having an affair and lying about it on a daily basis to the spouse. That nearly stopped my session, as the men and women began looking at each other trying to decide, "Is this you? Did you write that?" It was quite a different beginning for my workshop.

Foster parents deal with lying behavior from their foster children on a daily basis, and some, I'm sure, will admit they encountered the same with their biological children. Children may be taught right from wrong, but often the connection between believing that a certain action is right and doing it is weak.

People may behave very honestly in certain situations and not so well in others. Different situations play into how honest and dishonest people are at times. For instance, would you ask for a child's ticket at the movies for 12-year-olds, when your child turned 13 few days before?

The behavior of lying is truly a challenge for foster/ adoptive parents. But there are underlying factors that motivate most of the behavior.

Foster parents use different methods to reach their foster children. Some try to persuade, some bribe, some threaten and some appeal to the child's good nature. But until we understand what what's going on in their lives, we may not ever reach them. We hate to think we are not making a difference with regard to a child's behavior, but sometimes we must realize that we can't win them all.

In working with children, we frequently try to change their behaviors. Before we can be successful at changing behaviors, we need to know what is motivating the behavior. To help us understand motivations behind some of the more challenging behaviors, I would like you to look at the five basic psychological needs that we are all born with.

- To Belong—The need to love and be loved
- To have Power—The need to be heard
- To have Freedom—The need to make choices, to be unrestrained
- To have Fun—The need for enjoyment, pleasure or amusement
- To be Cared for—The need to be nurtured, to be safe and protected

Foster children are also attempting to get control of their lives and get their needs met. Most of them have learned to survive in the environment that they were living in before they came to you. They have not learned that there are more acceptable ways to get their needs met. Your task as a foster parent is to identify needs and teach appropriate skills. This can prove to be a challenge because the children with whom you are working are reluctant to let go of the familiar, problematic methods they've always used to get their needs met in the past.

A lot of the children coming into care have not had parental warmth, nor have they learned the values that they need to progress in a positive way. Children need that connection to identify with a parent who is caring and to be able to pattern values and behavior after the parent. They need to value the approval of the parent. Most of our foster children's lives have been in direct contrast to that.

They have grown up on their own without the warmth and acceptance of loving parents. They have grown up without the appropriate level of control and without any encouragement to help develop moral thinking.

You can start out by using such things as "time out" for small children. Advance upward as children get older, using more rules and giving more instructions and consequences. As they get older, you can use reasoning. The degree of parental control needs to keep pace with the child's increased need for freedom. Children should be encouraged to use self-control and judgment as much as possible in order to develop these abilities and to shape their behavior and moral thinking.

Parents who do not interact very often with their children have little influence over their children's behavior or developing values. Children today are exposed to many different and conflicting values. In order for parents to have a significant influence on helping foster children develop morality and the right values, they must have regular interaction and involvement.

What is happening today in homes? Parents are becoming less and less involved with their children. Children are watching more television, playing more video games and spending less and less time with family. Meal time is a rushed event with little or no discussion. Most of the time, meal is a pick up something and run about your business event. This seems to decrease the power of parents to influence their children and increases the power of peers to influence. As a result, more kids are coming into care. We often reinforce lying without even realizing it. Any time a child escapes punishment through lying, the lying behavior is strengthened. Have you ever promised a child that if they will tell you the truth you won't punish them? They'll tell you something, anything, truth or not, just to escape punishment.

Foster parents have a tremendous challenge though simply knowing how to deal with bad behaviors, giving the proper control or consequences just at the right time and teaching the child moral values.

Lying Behavior – Part II

Foster children use lying as a way of protecting themselves. Typically, these children have gone through abuse, neglect and have not resolved a family issue such as divorce, frequent moves, sexual abuse or other issues creating the removal from their homes. Lying has become a way of protecting themselves either from a real or perceived threat. For these children, lying turns into a habit that is used in other situations even when it is not needed. This pattern must be broken and the child taught a more appropriate defense mechanism. You need to learn to look at most lying as a call for help and hear the words beneath the lie.

Foster children have different types of lying behaviors that we need to consider and evaluate for the possible underlying reasons. One of the lying behaviors that foster children might use can be described as the fantasy lie, which is more daydreaming, flight of the imagination, wishful thinking or defensive escape from unpleasant reality. They communicate their daydreams as though they were reality.

A foster child after her first home visit states that her mother took her shopping and bought her new clothes. When asked by the other foster girls where the new clothes were, she responded, "I left them at my house until I go home. Then they will still be new." She didn't go shopping. She was just fantasizing about what she wished would have happened because her mother did not show up for the visit and she was only with her grandmother.

Fabrication is making up or creating stories just to get attention. Some children, who know the difference between truthfulness and lying, tell elaborate stories which appear believable. Children or adolescents usually relate these stories with enthusiasm because they receive a lot of attention as they tell the lie. Subsequently, the more attention they get, the bigger the "whopper" becomes.

One of my foster sons was always telling his friends that the reason he was in foster care was that his father was an executive working in another country and would be coming to get him when school was out. He got the attention of others, but the truth was that his dad was serving time in prison.

Social or white lies misrepresent the truth to spare hurt feelings of others or to avoid uncomfortable social conflicts—telling others what we think they want to hear. I think we may all be guilty of this. Husbands are often found in this type of a social falsehood when his wife asks if a dress looks good on her. How many men will say "no?" Or how about thanking someone for that wonderful gift you received when you wonder what you're going to do with it? Foster children are also guilty of the social lies used to gain or keep friendships.

Compulsive, uncontrollable or pathological lying is lying that occurs frequently, as a habit or an automatic reaction. This is often done to cover or hide some delinquent act or deed. If a child develops this pattern of lying, then professional help may be needed. Evaluation by a child and adolescent psychiatrist would help the child and foster parent understand the lying behavior and would also provide insight to the more serious underlying problem.

Younger children often exaggerate. Some of the pre-school stories are more a sign of a creative imagination than actual lying. We should take this into consideration and not consider this as a lying behavior.

There are many reasons that kids lie. Some may do it to escape criticism or punishment. The child may want to escape your displeasure, disapproval or anger, as well as to escape consequences or discipline.

I remember when my mom would get upset with me, I felt I needed to do anything to avoid her punishment. I lied so she would not take action against me for what I had done.

Most children come into care with low self-esteem and try to cover up for their low self-worth by exaggerating the truth or fabricating stories to gain status. This might happen if parental expectations are unrealistic or too high. An example would be one of foster children's report cards. My birth child came in with A's and B's, but the highest grade for the foster child was C's and D's. He would always tell me that the teacher said she had given him the wrong grade and that she said it would be changed before the next card came out. He wanted me to be as proud of him and not compare him with my daughter.

Children may also lie to escape unpleasant reality, using lying to escape or to make their denial defense stronger. For example, a child who has been sexually abused may repeatedly lie about his/her experience in order to avoid painful memories. Repeated lying about this seems to alter the painful reality somewhat and makes it seem as if it didn't happen. It's painful to go back and remember such a traumatic experience. They are reluctant to let foster parent and others know the real truth about what has happened in their life and often cast blame on a friend or family member.

Some children lie to imitate parents who lie. They may have lived in a home where the birth parents use lying as a daily reaction to many of their problems. "Now this is what we're going to say and don't tell anyone what really happened." We, too, need to be careful how we role model in front of our foster children. All too often we may not realize that we are unconsciously displaying the wrong side of truth. What messages do you suppose children get when they hear us say, "You answer the phone, and if it's Mrs. Busybody, tell her that I am not at home."

Okay, mom, you are standing right there by the phone. What example are you setting for your children?

Children may lie to seek revenge for unfair treatment. They know that they cannot express anger directly, so they may use lying as a means of discharging aggression, such can be seen where there are children coming from different homes with the feeling they have to fight for attention and get revenge on other children in the home through tattling, gossiping and bad mouthing. Becoming the troublemaker in the family is often a way of punishing foster parents, while at the same time a child may feel that he/she is keeping one step head of other children in the home.

Children lie to gain power through controlling others. Children who have been repeatedly mistreated and caused to feel powerless may use this reason for lying as a source of power. They control others' attitudes and actions to boost their own feeling of power. They feel they have no ability to effect change in their own life or to determine what happens to them, and they may attempt to let out their feelings of powerlessness through an unusual need to control or dominate others.

Then some lie to maintain secrecy, to protect self and to keep others from becoming involved in their business. They have experienced mistreatment and have come to distrust others. They wish to avoid intimacy. One of the hardest things that I've had to do as a foster parent is to reach out to a child who did not trust me, who was often caught lying in an effort to keep me out of their life.

The most serious reason for lying is when foster children use lying to cover up very serious problems. These can include drug addition, where they have been, who they were with, what they were doing, how they got money to spend and how they spent it. Stealing is another troubling area with which many foster parents are confronted.

When you are dealing with children who display lying behaviors, remember to always evaluate the underlying reason behind the lying first. Get to the core of the problem to correct it and then you will begin to see results.

Lying Behavior–Part III

Dealing with the lying behavior is a difficult problem, and there's no magical fix. We begin by realizing that the problem does not have an easy answer and that it's very common in foster children. Foster parents should always look at the problem on a case-by-case basis. What worked for one child may not work for another.

In my research on lying behavior in children, it was noted that ignoring the behavior is a good technique to deal with it. But even though you may try to ignore it, you should listen. I know that there are some small lies that will grow into big ones if left alone. As you grow to know your child, you will be able to determine which ones to ignore and which ones to address.

We should not label our foster children or verbally or mentally brand them as liars. We need to handle this situation very carefully. Foster children often are watching and waiting for our response. They observe how we handle their problem and wait to see if we are going to pass judgment on them.

Share with the child what is important and what is not. They may be searching for an answer and need to hear from you. Help the child think through the consequences for each situation when they are caught in lying. Give the child an opportunity to state their own method about how to deal with the situation or problem created by the lying and listen to how they plan to correct the problem. If their plan is unreasonable or unwise, you can recommend another method that might work better. If we allow the child to go through this decision-making process, hopefully, the child will soon figure out the right way to handle the situation and understand that lying is not the answer.

For young children who demonstrate excessive fantasy behavior, attention can be given to them by gently directing them to the difference between fantasy and reality with comments such as "that's make-believe, isn't it?" Have a serious talk and discuss the difference between make believe and reality in addition to a discussion about lying and telling the truth. It is normal for children four to five years of age to often make up stories and tell tall tales because they enjoy hearing stories and making up stories for fun.

A successful method that I've used is to play the opposite game. You buy two different flavors of ice creams. Ask the child which flavor they would like and then give them the opposite. If they complain, then explain to them, "I know that you often do not tell me the truth, and I felt you might not be telling me the truth now. I just knew you meant the other." You can also ask if they want to stay up late. If they say "yes," then send them to bed immediately and explain that you knew they really meant just the opposite.

Be prepared for tears and tantrums, but just keep smiling and saying how sorry you are that you never know when they are telling the truth. Add that tomorrow maybe things will be different, and you will believe them. The next day, ask the same thing but this time, give them what they ask for. You will be surprised the impression this will make on the child.

Most of our children come to us with low self-esteem. We need to look at the symptoms with a child who is struggling with frequent lying, not the problem. Parents should make a special effort to make truth telling safe, something of which the child can be proud. Focus on giving the child praise daily for appropriate actions or good qualities, which will help the child to feel better. A child who feels good about him/herself will feel less need to lie.

Keeping a chart on the refrigerator has also been helpful. Foster parents can put a star for truth and either remove it or have a list for a known lie. This works well with younger children, especially if they get extra money added to their allowance as a reward.

Sometimes we find ourselves questioning our foster children who have had a history of lying to us even at times that they are telling us the truth.

A foster child often told me he did not have homework, but his report card and calls from the teacher had always proved otherwise. One day, he came in and told me he left his homework sheet on the bus. Due to past experiences, I questioned his honesty. I went to the bus garage and found it there by his seat. Did he leave it there on purpose? I don't know, but I felt he should be rewarded for telling the truth.

A story is told of a butcher in a small grocery store. He and his foster son were just about to close for the night when a customer came in and wanted to buy a chicken. The butcher went to the back and came out with the last chicken he had left in his shop. He weighed the chicken and told the lady how much it weighed. She thought for a moment and then said, "I really wanted a larger one." The shopkeeper wanting to sell that last chicken went to the back and came back with the same chicken.

He weighed it and told the lady, "Now this one weights a pound more than the other one."

"Fine," she said, "I'll take them both."

Watching this entire event was his foster son and what a message this sent to him about honesty and his foster dad's role modeling.

Children are like video recorders. They take in everything they see and hear, then play it back. It is very important that we model truthful behavior for them at all times.

Lying is the single most common problem among foster children and is something that comes as a rude awakening for many new foster parents. It's very important that we understand that these children come from a world where lying is common and, for many, has become a means of survival. This behavior is often difficult to detect and hard to change for many reasons. Remember, it's a behavior that all children and adults commit at some level. When it becomes the natural thing to do and is done frequently, then it can be defined as a problem behavior. Lying often causes a strong negative reaction from foster parents, and the mistrust creates added conflicts. Negative reactions restrict us from understanding the child's underlying problems.

We can truly say that dogs bark, cats meow, and children often lie. Your neighbor's kid will lie, birth kids lie, and yes, so do foster children. This behavior can frustrate foster parents, but hopefully we will be able to add some additional tools to put in the bag of tricks we are required to use as parents.

Stealing Behavior

I often took my foster children with me when I went shopping. One afternoon, I decided to go into town with all five of my children. I had a six-year-old boy that had been with me since he was five months old. He was a beautiful little boy whose mother had experienced a series of problems with drugs and alcohol while carrying him. He had come to us in a very neglected and undernourished condition but seemed to be improving daily.

We went into a store where they had a playroom and toys for children to play with while their parents shopped. When I got ready to leave, I noticed that my six-year-old had already gone out to the van. I found him hidden in the very back. Quite naturally, one of the other children told me he had something that he had taken from the store—a truck from the playroom. I made him get out. I went with him and had him return the truck to the clerk and tell her he was sorry he took it. I had hoped this would show him what he'd done was wrong. Later that evening, I had a family meeting and a discussion on the subject of taking something that was not yours with all the foster children.

Stealing is a behavior that can be quite upsetting to foster parents, but the fact that stealing may be a common problem with foster and adopted children doesn't make that behavior any less upsetting. Stealing causes more concern because it may happen outside the home and will affect other people. Once we recognize that this has occurred, we may feel that the child is lost and doomed to a life of crime and incarceration. This is certainly not always the case, and we should be relieved to know that the vast majority of children who occasionally steal grow up to be law-abiding citizens. Foster parents need to recognize some of the reasons foster children steal and ways in which to deal with the behavior.

Stealing and lying behaviors cannot be separated as the two often go hand in hand. If a child is stealing, somewhere you will find that lying behavior is involved.

In most cases it doesn't help to make a big issue at first and treat the foster child as if he/she has committed a major offense. It could be a first-time thing, and it is very important to handle the situation correctly. You don't want to humiliate the child, but it should be made very clear here that such behavior is unacceptable and is not to be repeated.

If a foster parent is absolutely sure that the child has stolen something, the child must be confronted. Question where the object came from and insist that it be restored to the rightful owner or restitution be made.

Foster children, in most cases, in their birth homes have not been taught the difference between borrowing and stealing. House rules must be given to children as they come into the home explaining that they need to ask before taking anyone's personal belongings. If the item is still taken after the person says, "No, you can't borrow it," reinforce that to take something without permission is stealing and consequences will be given. We have to teach and enforce respect for other people's possession.

Small children aged from one to three years occasionally pick up things that don't belong to them, but their intention is not to steal. This is an age of generally self-centeredness, and it is not a good idea to punish children that young or to call this stealing. Instead, this is an excellent time for foster parents to begin teaching about ownership and the concept that stealing is wrong. At that age, children are too young to comprehend the concept of possession and that something could belong exclusively to someone. They have yet to develop the concepts of "yours" and "mine," so when they see something they like, they feel it's all right to take it. If your three-year-old foster child walks off with something that belongs to a playmate, don't overreact. Simply explain that the item belongs to their friend and that she would like to have it back. This is a common, normal behavior in preschool aged children.

I have read the book: "Trial to Triumph- One Foster Parent's Journey" by Betty Hastings, author, foster parent and former foster child.

After reading the book I have the following comments to make as to how it relates to my continuing commitment as a foster parent:
(This must be a paragraph expressing thoughts on the book, will it be helpful or not,)

_____

_____

_____

_____

_____

_____

_____

_____

_____

I therefore request that the allowed three (3) hours credit be applied to my record as approval for DCS training requirement.

_____   _____
Foster Parent's Name   Date

To receive credit, each parent must complete a form to receive credit hours.

By the time a child reaches the age of six to adolescence and begins to take items that do not belong to them, most probably they are aware that what they are doing is not right. By this time, their conscience has developed. When children in this age group take something that does not belong to them they tend to be secretive about it. Once children begin to show an understanding of these concepts, parents should begin setting limits on stealing behaviors and providing consequences when such behavior occurs. Make sure you know what you're talking about before you accuse a child and have evidence to show you're correct. Keep your eyes open for unexplained items that appear in their possession.

Stealing may occur in children no matter how many possessions your child has, so giving them everything is not a successful approach to stopping stealing. The child I took shopping that took the truck at the age of six ended up with a history of continued stealing. We tried buying items that we felt he was interested in, things that we felt might help to remove his desire to take items from others, but we never got it out of him. In his teen years he spent time in juvenile detention for theft, and then later a drug problem only caused him to spend more time in detention for stealing.

Most of the time, if stealing persists through childhood and adolescence and is not corrected, the chances of the youth becoming a serious adult offender are high.

Some of the children that we take into care come from homes where respect for others' property was not taught. Birth parents or older siblings frequently stole things without being punished, so they have learned to steal by example. Their parents model stealing behaviors as a way of life. It has been found that these children had only distant relationships with their birth parents with very little positive interaction and supervision. Often they had a rejecting mother, received little or no discipline, or were allowed to go out and wander the neighborhood at all hours of the day and night. Often, that birth mother did not know where they were, and they had no curfew or set time for meals.

Children who steal often have the same problems as children who had lying behaviors. We also find that they have poor problem-solving skills, lower levels of moral reasoning, difficulty in viewing situations from the perspective of others, difficulty empathizing with the feelings of others and exhibit very poor relationships with other children.

It is for these reasons that it is so hard to find foster parents for teens. They have been in their birth homes almost all of their young lives and have developed some of these characteristics that foster parents do not know how to deal with.

Withstanding to the End

Foster children have many problems
Sometimes big and sometimes small
Foster parents must be willing and prepared
To be able to face them all
But there's one behavior that strains
And works on patience, too
It's stealing and lying behavior
Often we don't know what to do
You certainly don't want to label a child a thief or liar
On the very first offense,
But we need to look, search for the core of the problem
In their own defense
You never know when you can help make a difference
In the life of the child
Let them know you love them
To help them through the trials
Foster parents may be able to see change
And accomplishment in the end
Not only to conquer lying and stealing behavior
But to gain a lifetime friend

Stealing Behavior – Part II

Perhaps one of the most bizarre incidents of a foster child stealing was a call that I received from the school regarding my fourth-grade foster son. It was after lunch and the children had gone into the bathroom to wash their hands before returning to the classroom. One of the students had removed his retainer from his mouth to clean. My foster son had taken the retainer and hidden it in his pocket. What possible reason would there be for this child to have taken this particular item?

There are many reasons why children steal, and I think it's very important for foster parents to search out what's behind this behavior.

Collecting valued objects is a natural instinct in children. It's common for young children to pick up things and bring them home after a visit to a friend's house. When this occurs, the child and the object should be brought back to the friend's along with an apology. Giving an explanation about why you are making the child do this could have a lasting impression.

I am not saying that every child who picks up something and doesn't return it is going to become a thief when they get older. I don't want to give that impression at all. But we can use the experience as a learning tool for the child regardless of how young they are.

Children often take items belonging to others just to satisfy their curiosity, as in the incident of the retainer being taken. Peer pressure can be very influential and sometimes results in "I'll show you I can," type incidents. Acts of stealing may be just to feel powerful, to gain attention, vent feelings of jealousy or even to get revenge. Foster children coming into care with very low self-esteem may exhibit stealing behavior for all of these reasons. They may feel justified because they have led deprived lives and are needy. Often, their material needs have not been satisfied. Hoarding food is certainly an example of this.

After examining the odor coming from my teenage foster son's bedroom, I once found the source of missing food from my pantry and refrigerator. It revealed vast amounts of food hidden under his bed and in the dresser drawers. Discussions repeatedly about this behavior didn't seem to work. Looking into his past revealed a background of padlocks that had been placed on the refrigerator door, which kept him from having his hunger satisfied. Placing a small refrigerator in the downstairs kitchen just outside his room and trying to keep those food items that I felt he would be most interested in having, helped some, but I don't know that I ever got rid of his desire to hoard food. I feel he always had the fear that one day, he would be denied food again.

The emotional hunger that exists because of the separation from the birth family often means these children are emotionally deprived and seek to feel worthwhile. Children who have been deprived of attention from their mother or who have not had someone they could depend on for help and support feel an overwhelming hunger for love. They often use alternate methods to get their needs met, such as stealing.

Foster children often come into our homes with a different concept of property. They've never learned the difference between what's mine and what's yours or to value ownership. One foster child was giving away some of the items in my home because his perception of the items was that we had money and could get more. Because he had more material possession than prior to coming to live with us, he thought he could give them away to gain friends.

A child may steal simply to assert him/herself and to rebel. Foster children often feel resentment toward being in foster care. They don't want to be there. They feel no one cares and because they can't always express their anger, they rebel by acting out and stealing. Stealing can also have its roots in feelings of fear, resentment or jealousy.

When children seldom keep what is stolen, but give it away instead, they may want to give gifts or money to others in order to gain their approval, attention and love. Loneliness and a lack of closeness to anyone is a great explanation for why children steal. They may have difficulty making friends and resort to stealing to buy the affection of peers or in an attempt to satisfy cravings for attention and affection.

Foster children need to receive an allowance if they are old enough to understand the concept of money. If they have their own money that they have worked for, they will be less likely to steal. They see other children having money and should not feel like they are deprived. Some children can't handle money, and only the foster parent will be able to determine if and how to handle lessons in money management and distribution.

I remember my teen years in foster care system. How I envied children who were able to buy that extra food item at lunch or buy things that I knew I couldn't have. I did not resort to stealing, but I felt so empty and deprived at times.

There are chores that can be given to earn a weekly allowance or maybe the state board payment requires your child to receive some type of allowance. But, if children do not have any money of their own to spend, it may open the door to the temptation to steal.

Taking drugs has become more and more widespread across our nation, and seemingly the age involved is getting younger and younger. Children and young adults steal and sell items in order to pay for their drug habits. If you find this to be true with a child that you're dealing with, it is suggested that you deal with the drug problem first because it is probably the core of the problem with stealing.

Any time a foster parent is dealing with a stealing behavior, it is very important that the parent seek out the underlying reason. Understanding the "why" will certainly help to resolve the problem.

I wish there were a magical wand I could offer to wave over the stealing problems with your foster child, but I haven't as of yet found any permanent fixes. I do have some suggestions that I would like for you to think about and perhaps consider the next time you have a suspicion that your foster child has a stealing behavior.

- Set aside time to teach your children about property rights and consideration of others
- Make an effort to give more recognition to the child as an important member of your family. This will be helpful if the child is stealing just to get attention.
- Explain how hard money is to earn, why it's important to have enough and why we can't just take it from others.
- Give children an allowance and let them open a bank account to teach them the importance of saving.
- Tell your child stealing is wrong and discuss the reasons why.
- Make it clear that this behavior is unacceptable within the family and within the
  community.

If you know without a doubt your child has stolen, you must handle the situation differently:

- Don't panic. Think through your actions
- Re-emphasize: Tell the child that stealing is wrong
- Return the object or pay for it
- Make sure the child does not benefit from the theft in any way
- Avoid lecturing, fussing and predicting future bad behavior or suggesting that the child is a bad person or a thief. Once the child has returned the item, do not bring it up again. Let the child begin have a clean slate. If it happens again, seek professional help.
- Remind the child that this behavior in unacceptable in your home, and you will not tolerate it.
- If stealing is persistent and recurring, seek professional help as it could be a sign or more serious problems. Get involved in the treatment plan. Help the child to establish trusting relationship and change toward healthier development.
- Involve the agency about all steps taken and keep your worker informed.
- Discuss and draw up a contract with your child.

- If it is a serious problem, such as stealing a car, call the police and your worker.

During all my years of fostering, I've experienced the loss of many items, including several large items that could not be recovered. I've had a new car stolen and demolished, a diamond ring and large amounts of money. I learned a great deal over the years, and I can relate to each of the reasons why foster children display the stealing behavior.

One of the most interesting thefts I had was a teenage girl placed in our home for emergency care for a few days. On the third day, she left to go to a group facility. The worker called me when they arrived there and asked me if I had a new thermos cup missing. It still had the tag on it. I had bought it the day before. When the child was questioned, she told them that I gave every child that came into my home something to take away with them. The worker also asked if I had an ID bracelet with "Betty" inscribed on it. They had found my ID bracelet and asked her about it. She said, "It's mine. Betty is my nickname."

When you have determined that your foster child's stealing has really become a problem, you may have to take more drastic action. Be sure your worker is aware of the precautions and actions that you are taking.

- Develop a plan for the future to keep the behavior from occurring again.
- Provide regular supervision, particularly if the child is suspected of past thefts.
- Establish a curfew. Tighten the reins on older children by making their curfew much earlier. Don't allow them to leave your sight without adult supervision. Drive them to school and even taken them to class if necessary. Tell them restrictions will be lifted when they prove they can be trusted.
- Have them check in regularly so that you know their whereabouts.
- Suspend their right to privacy until they learn to respect the belongings of others.

- Treat stealing seriously.
- Make the child return or pay for the item. Have him/her apologize and work off the amount of the item or take it out of his/her allowance.
- Give extra chores or writing and math practice
- Suspend privileges for a reasonable time.
- Bring the child to visit a local jail if the problem gets out of control. Talk with your worker and if it's okay, have a deputy talk to the child, maybe take him/her to a cell and show the child how handcuffs work.
- Again, make a contract with your child. Explain the contract and make it for a certain length of time. Let the child help you write it. Make sure that it is signed by both parties and that a copy is given to the child and to your worker. Do not back down. Administer consequences if the contract is broken.

In a lying/stealing training session I sat through some time ago, a foster parent said, "I don't have to wait to find out if my new foster child steals when he first comes into my home. I just put four quarters on top of the dresser and if they are still there the next morning, then I know that the child is going to be okay and won't steal."

Can you believe that? We should never tempt these children. Don't ever leave your wallet or cigarettes in view. Considering their backgrounds, some children can't resist the temptation.

As role models, we are teaching our foster children with everything we do. When we come home with stationary or pens from the office or brag about a mistake at the supermarket checkout counter, lessons about honesty will be a lot harder for the foster child to understand. We want to be very careful modeling honesty.

How you handle an incident will definitely affect a child in his future life, even after they leave your home. A stealing incident that occurred with two of my teenage foster boys and our action made an impression on one of the children.

My husband was a used car dealer and took a lot of pride in his work.

He also enjoyed working with boys in care. He had just purchased a late model used car. With the help of the two teenage foster sons, he worked diligently to get it cleaned and ready to sell. He had a customer coming the next morning to purchase the car.

In the middle of the night, I heard the sound of the car's motor running, and I ran to the carport door just in time to see the tail lights as it left the driveway. Horrified and extremely excited, we ran to the bedroom of the teens. Their beds were empty. We realized that not only had they taken the car, but they had also taken money from my purse.

Later, I asked one of the boys why they went into my purse when Charles always had more money in his wallet than I carried. The response was, "We didn't want to get into Pop's money. We knew he would punish us." What did they think I would do? Reward them?"

After we called the police and the worker, we listened to the scanner and knew that the boys were doing some fast joy riding. It was not long before they were stopped, and according to the scanner, the car had been wrecked. The boys had run off the road into a big ditch, destroyed the car, but fortunately, they were not hurt. Since one of the boys had been with us for three years and the other had been placed in our home as an emergency placement, we felt that the boy who had been with us had been led into stealing the car. He didn't deserve the full punishment of jail and to be labeled as a juvenile delinquent. We paid his bond and took him back home.

Since this was not the first offense for the other child, he remained in jail to face a court hearing for his actions. We never regretted making this decision because of the impression it made on the child we took home. In his later adult life, the child we took home often reminded us about it and expressed appreciation for our decision.

You may wonder what you can do to change your child's behavior. A point to remember is that the child must want to change. You cannot do it for them. As foster parents, we must realize that transforming lying or stealing behaviors takes time. Look for improvement in the behavior rather than a quick fix or a complete elimination of it.

Do not expect dramatic improvement in these behaviors in a short period of time. With our foster children we must be patient and consistent and commit ourselves to fighting these behaviors at every opportunity. Fostering is hard work. It requires patience, knowledge and an understanding of the child's problems. Go into this with your eyes open and use every opportunity you have to teach honesty. Create your own methods to deal with problems when they occur. It may help to count to 10 before speaking and acting.

Remember you may be holding the future of the child in your hand, and often the child is carefully watching your reaction and how you handle the behavior. Foster parents can make a difference.

Fostering Teens – I Can Handle It

Even if you are not a parent of a teenager, you will deal with teens in your life at one time or another. They may be the neighbors' kids, your brother or sister or kids at church. There are so many troubled teenagers today, and it's not just the ones in foster care. Think about it, our teenagers are our leaders tomorrow. Considering some of the ones I've had placed in my home, that is a scary thought!

Not all teens are created equal. They are each completely different individuals, and most of them have to be handled on an individual basis. Even my own three biological children were very different.

The word teenager conjures up an image of a wild and reckless young person whose main purpose in life is to rebel against his or her parents or care takers. But every teen does not fit into this category. It's normal to worry, whether the teen is a foster child or your biological child.

Are the issues affecting teenagers really that different now than they were years ago? Their issues include:

- Sexual pressure
- Self-image problems
- A need to fit in
- Academic pressure
- Broken homes
- A different world from their parents

- Drugs
- Television
- Less family oriented society
- Outside intervention
- No spiritual direction
- Peer Pressure

I'm sure you will agree with me that some of the things listed are creating more problems today. Or it could be that we are simply more aware of the problems.

It seems more and more difficult to find foster homes for teens today. We've labeled teens in foster care and stereotyped them as different from normal kids. They are viewed as being dysfunctional, bad and unruly just because they are in care. All too often we feel that there's no hope for that teen in care. They are difficult, and it's not worth the effort to help fight to make a difference in their lives.

One teenager's response to this was, "I consider myself to be strong and fight for myself," he said, "I realized that besides God, there are very few people fighting for me. I know that there are people out there who don't believe I can make it, so I'm determined to prove them wrong." This was the attitude that I had as a teen in my years in care.

When a call comes asking for placement of a teenage, I know that we all have different reactions. It may be curiosity about what did they do to cause themselves to be in care. Foster parent may feel that they would like to try it but are nervous about it. They worry how it will affect the other children in the home. Some just immediately say, "No! I don't do teenagers and that's the final answer!"

There are those who do feel empathy and compassion and open their home, particularly when the teen has been placed into care due to a death in his/her family. I've walked that path and experienced loneliness, despair, anguish and being isolated from family and friends. Foster parents who have been foster children themselves are quicker to offer their home for placement. They understand the concept of wanting to belong to a family, needing love and wanting to be recognized with having the potential to become a success in life.

If we were to look at the reasons that teens come into care, often it's no different than the reasons younger children are placed. There are the abandoned, the abused, the neglected teenagers. Truancy and problems that parents were unable to cope are also causes for placements. It seems to me that the truancy problem would be the responsibility of the parents who simply need some special direction and guidance in parenting skills. But often the judge sees fit to place these kids in foster care.

Statistics show that nearly one third of all foster kids come from poor families and a vast majority is non-white. Children who have experienced family violence and parental addictions have sometimes formed non-secure attachments and find it difficult to bond with their foster parents. One third or more of the teens in foster care have been in three or more placements. The greater number of placements a child has, the more difficult it is to establish a good relationship with foster parents. Each move sets a child back at least six months and puts them behind academically.

When a 15-year-old boy was placed in my home, he immediately told me that he had already had 15 placements and would not be in my home long. I informed him that he had never experienced living in my home. I told him that I had been a foster child and could handle most situations. He came expecting failure. How it always hurt to hear such defeat in a child before there was even a chance for a successful placement.

One of the most disturbing placements that I've had in my home was a young teenage girl and her baby. Pregnancy with our teenage girls is a growing problem today. My heart went out to the young mother when she told me that she had asked to be placed in foster care with her baby. She did not want him to be raised in the same drug riddled abusive environment to which she had been exposed.

Keeping mothers and baby has its positive note. One, you get to give parental direction to the mother. Second, you have the advantages of having a baby in the home, but you can get their mom to get up in the middle of the night to tend to diapers, crying, etc. while you quietly oversee.

Not all teenagers come into care because of their delinquent behavior or something that they did. Circumstance forces some into care, and they deserve an opportunity to better their condition. Many success stories have come from foster care, including Marilyn Monroe, Edgar Allen Poe, Malcolm X, and Keith Bulluck from the Tennessee Titans.

I suppose that I could say that I have a success story, as well. But while in care, I felt there was no one to believe in me. I definitely felt alone, and with five placements it was as though no one cared. I graduated from high school with no support or help from my placements and without an opportunity to go to college. I wanted to go so badly, but I didn't know how to even begin looking or applying for grants. That still hurts to this day. I, like so many other foster children, felt that there were those who did not think I was able, capable or deserving of a brighter future.

The teenage placements can be very trying for foster parents who are willing to step out and take the teen into their home, but it can be very difficult and frustrating for the teen, too. Some will irritate their foster parents by learning what buttons to push, but the truth is that they are hurting and reaching out for love. They need attention and help to reach a better understanding of their life and future.

Fostering Teens – Guidelines

To understand the total picture when dealing with fostering teens, we need to consider the development stages of the adolescence — the transitional stage of human development in which a juvenile matures into an adult. During this time, there are dramatic changes in the body, along with development in a person's psychology and academic career. These years can be as challenging as they are exciting.

"Who am I?" and "Where do I fit in?" are common questions teens ask. Being in foster care often adds to this confusion. Teenagers can become truly discouraged while they work on trying to build their self esteem. Teens may question themselves in many areas as their bodies develop. They may even have questions about same sex crushes. Be prepared to explain that this does not mean that he or she is destined to be homosexual.

After puberty, a boy's strength continues to develop, while teen girls tend to level out. Research has shown that regular physical activity helps improve strength and coordination in both sexes.

The teenage years can be a trying time for both the teenager and foster families. One of the most difficult things a foster parent can face with a teenager is that teenagers typically think they are always right. This is not just a foster care teen problem, but it happens with all teenagers. With a foster child, problems can become magnified, which complicates things even more. It' not surprising that disagreements between foster parents and teens occur.

You have to constantly ask yourself if the problem is because the teen is in foster care or if it could be normal teenage rebellion. I'm reminded daily of this with my adopted son. I have to ask if his behavior is normal or does it stem from the fact that he's adopted and was in foster care with multiple placements before coming to me.

Are the following behaviors normal or just related to teens in foster care?

- Losing one's temper
- Arguing with adults
- Actively defying requests
- Refusing to follow rules
- Deliberately annoying other people
- Blaming others for one's own mistakes or misbehavior
- Being touchy, easily annoyed or angered, resentful, spiteful or vindictive

Most of us can answer that question immediately. Most teenagers experience these behaviors. Here's what you can do to help the situation:

- Love unconditionally and show it
- Get counseling when necessary, both family and individual to determine underlying issues and learn strategies for behavior change
- Join support groups to help guide and empower parents with other foster parents whose been there and done the work
- Attend special training classes to learn ways of providing consistency, structure and a positive, less stressful home environment
- Open lines of Communication — listening and valuing adolescent ideas is what promotes effective communication. Most time we find that we are too busy with work, community, church and even our other children and home responsibilities to effectively listen.
- Talk about morals and ethical behavior. Pass along a sense of values. Talk about what is right and wrong, appropriate and inappropriate behavior. Give them time to respond and listen to their response.

- Deal always with what is important. Don't make an issue about minor things that do not directly affect yours or your child's safety or violates rules, such as a messy room, unwashed hair and clothes in some cases. Save your thunder for more important concerns.

- Be consistent and hold your ground. There will be times that your teen won't like what you say or will act as though they don't even like you. Being their friend should not be your primary role during the time they are in foster care in your home. It's important to resist the urge to win their favor or try too hard to please them if they are not right in action or decisions.

- Avoid arguments. Arguing only fuels hostility, and it doesn't get you heard. Never try to reason with an upset teenager. Wait until tempers have cooled off before trying to sort out a disagreement.

- Be a role model and provide guidance in all that you do.

- Stayed involved in teen's every day life and include teen in decision making

- Make foster home comfortable and make the child feel like a welcome part of the family

- Be honest and truthful always.

- Build trust gradually so your teenager will feel comfortable talking with you about sensitive subjects. Talk in a safe place that is safe for you and the teen (understanding that the worker is always kept aware of conversations).

- Discuss sexual orientation. Teens may question themselves in many areas as their body develops, and they may question even having same sex crushes. Be prepared to explain that this does not mean that he or she is destined to be homosexual. Explain that, in some cases, these feelings grow stronger over time rather than fade away.

- Negotiate with the teen a Home Rules Contact and let him/her help prepare the contract. You will be surprised how hard they can be on themselves when it comes to following rules. Do not back down from the rules. Write, Discuss, Agree, Sign, Carry Through.

Home Rules Contract

For the_____ family

This contract shall be from date: _____ to _____.

All family members, whose signatures are present on this document below, are in agreement with and will follow the rules and consequences of this Home Rules Contract as listed:

1. (list rule) _____

Consequence if rule is broken: _____

Privilege if rule is not broken within the contract period: _____

_____

Signatures of family members:

_____   _____
Foster Dad   Foster Mom

_____   _____
Foster Child   Date

You can add as many rules as you feel child can handle. Make sure that it's completed, signed and child gets a copy.

A man was exploring caves by the seashore. In one of the caves he found a canvas bag with a bunch of hardened clay balls. It was like someone had rolled clay balls and left them out in the sun to bake.

They didn't look like much, but they intrigued the man so he took the bag out of the cave with him. As he strolled along the beach, he would throw the clay balls one at a time out into the ocean as far as he could.

He thought little about it, until he dropped one of the clay balls and it cracked open on a rock. Inside was a beautiful, precious stone!

Excited, the man started breaking open the remaining clay balls. Each contained a similar treasure. He found thousands of dollars worth of jewels in the 20 or so clay balls he had left. Then it struck him.

He had been on the beach a long time. He had thrown maybe 50 or 60 of the clay balls with their hidden treasure into the ocean waves. Instead of thousands of dollars in treasure, he could have taken home tens of thousands, but he had just thrown it away!

I can relate this to teens today. We're asked to take one and we know the stigma that goes with teens. We see the external clay vessel. It doesn't look like much from the outside. We often don't feel they have a chance. But often we have not taken the time to find the treasure that might be hidden inside that person.

I believe that there is a treasure in each and every one of us. If we take the time to get to know that person, understand their problems, step inside that of their life with them, slowly the clay may begin to peel away and the brilliant gem begins to shine forth.

Someone once sent me 10 reasons why you should foster a teenager.

1. There are no formula, diapers, bottles or burp rags required.
2. You get to sleep through the night or at least you don't have to wake up to a crying infant.
3. They will move out sooner because hey will age out or foster care.
4. They can program cell phones and DVD players and teach you how to use the computer.
5. They will keep you updated on the latest fashions and trends.

6. They can often get their permits and drive you places.
7. You don't just get a placement, you can get a friend.
8. They can pick up after themselves and do their own laundry.
9. They can help you teach kindness, understanding and how to be empathetic.
10. They need someone to help them share their achievements and holidays.

Foster kids are our kids. They deserve an opportunity to succeed in life, even though they have been removed from their home. There is a great need for foster parents willing to give that teen needing a home a chance to grow, develop and have a brighter future. To give a teenager a new start in life in a healthy and safe environment may seem like a challenge for foster parents but can be gratifying and rewarding in the end.

You don't have to be perfect to foster a teenager. There are thousands of teens in foster care who would love to put up with you. Many are waiting for someone to give them understanding and give them the confidence necessary for a bright future.

You could have a future Malcolm X or an Edgar Allen Poe in your home. Remember, we were once teenagers, too.

Working with Birth Parents

Foster parents don't always want to work with birth parents. There seems to be a stigma about dealing with parents who have abused, neglected and abandoned their children. In our homes, we are offering these children a safe environment and trying to help them turn their life around. Now we're being told that we've going to be dealing with the same people who put them into this foster care situation. I think that that is a big reason why foster parents aren't interested in this particular subject.

Another important reason for not wanting to work with the birth parents is that we do not really know how to deal with the relationship with birth parents. Here we are, the parents filling in for birth mom and dad. We may feel that we do not have the skills and the qualifications to know what to do or what to say to birth parents. Temporarily, we're replacing mom and dad in the eyes of the birth parents, and it becomes difficult for many foster parents as well as birth parents to know how to deal with this situation.

I had a 16-year-old placed in our home due to truancy. His mom, uneducated and somewhat handicapped, was not in control in their home. He took care of her and the house, but he would not get up and go to school. When he was placed in our home, he followed me around the house asking all kinds of questions about cooking and housekeeping, but he had no interest in anything my husband did or in helping him outside.

He got to go home on weekends. When his mom and her friend came to pick him up on Friday, she would not even look at me as they drove into my drive. The same thing happened when she brought him back on Sunday night. The worker kept telling me to try to help out because Billy would be going home when school was out. She said his mom really loved him.

One day while he was sitting in the kitchen watching me, I told him he needed to learn something about preparing a meal. I started him out making cornbread. He watched, made it a few times that week and then went home on Friday evening as usual. When he came back on Sunday evening, I noticed that his mom looked at me and smiled. Surprised, I couldn't believe that she had looked at me, much less smiled! When Billy came in, he said to me, "My mom said to tell you thanks for showing me how to make cornbread. She had me make three skillets of cornbread to last until I go back home next weekend."

I was on a roll. I decided the next week I would show him how to make chicken and dumplings. So, I made them the easy way by boiling the chicken, pulling the meat off the bone, adding it with pinched up biscuits and dropping them in the broth.

When she came and picked him up that next weekend, his mom was smiled at me again, and when she brought him back on Sunday she waved and waved. I asked how the weekend went. Billy replied, "She was so happy. We went out and bought five chickens, and I made five pans of chicken and dumplings. I also made cornbread so they would have something to eat all week."

After that young man left my home, his mom called me one day, and said, "Miss Mom," (she didn't even know my name). "I just want to thank you for keeping my Billy. We're gonna eat good now."

We're seeing a new day dawning in the role of foster parents and the work they do with birth parents. We are now seeing foster parents co-leading in pre-service training and serving on state appointed committees. In some states, meetings are now held at the state office with foster parents in attendance.

Personally, I have served in my state on the governor's appointed Children's Cabinet and also on the Supreme Court Improvement Committee. Foster parents are taking on more major roles in the child welfare system today.

It makes great sense to me for foster parents to take a more active part in the foster care system, as all involved are members of a team working toward improving the life of that child in care. It is certainly a strong bond that the child has with the birth family and to successfully help the future of the child, foster parents need to be involved with the birth parents. Who else knows about the child except those who are with the child 24 -7? Who helps prepare for the child's return home by being a part of the team working in the best interest of the child? As foster parents, our role is to care for the child on every level, which includes becoming involved in the child welfare system.

We all have had some event or perhaps something in our lives that might create embarrassment if it became public knowledge. We may think that our families are different, but there is some dysfunction present in all families. Families are alike in that we all have skeletons hidden in our closets. This should help us understand and have more empathy when it comes to dealing with birth families and their problems. When we work with those who have had their children removed by the court system, over time we can understand that there may be hope for change in their lives and the opportunity for the child to safely return home.

We often need to examine our feelings regarding birth parents. Sometimes foster parents have a great deal of negative feelings in dealing with birth parents, and those barriers keep us from working successfully with them. Often we have feelings that they just simply don't care about their children. Sometimes it's hard to work with them because they often blame the system for all their problems and have a tendency to lie, to deny the true picture. They can also be very uncooperative, harassing or negative toward foster parents. In those instances, foster parents feel that the birth parents don't deserve to have their children back.

I know there have been some very negative incidents with birth parents. I've had some that I don't want to remember. Once, we went to pick up a placement, and soon after we got home, the worker called. She said she didn't mean to alarm us, but the birth mom had called the department and threatened to burn the home where the child had been placed. Birth mom had said that if she could not have him, no one could. This wouldn't have concerned me, but I had noticed that his mom had followed us home and had been riding around our house. I don't believe we slept too well that evening.

But there can be some positive experiences with birth parents, such as my experience with Billy and his mom. My story helps me remember how important it is to work with birth parents. Sometimes, it's the simple things that make the biggest impression. Many birth parents want to get their lives back together so they can bring their children home. Some are appreciative of the help and service foster parents provide to their children and are cooperative. They follow the guidelines provided to them in order to improve their situations. I have worked with parents who never intended to be bad parents and just needed direction and help in learning how to be good parents. There are even some that build good positive relationships with the foster parents and continue to have contact after the child comes home.

What works for one, may not work for another. Remember that each case must be handled on an individual basis to determine what is in the best interest of everyone involved.

What a gratifying feeling it is to see a child return home with the birth parent. It's even better when the birth parent shows appreciation for the work the foster parent did. The goal is to remember that this is all about the child's happiness and safety.

Working with Birth Parents – Part II

Foster care is temporary and reunification with birth parents is the highest priority. This often requires hard work, and it places great responsibility on the foster parents and workers, as well. We must be a team with the same goal in mind.

One very important thing to stress is that foster parents have a tremendous impact on their foster children simply by the feelings they have and by speaking positively a about the birth parent in front of the child. Before we can work in cooperation with birth parents, we really have to want to. Foster children can pick up negative feelings so easily and can tell when we don't want their birth parents in the picture. They may already have a difficult time understanding why they're not in their own home, and one of the most important concerns of a child in care is loss. Any loss is always painful because of its immediate impact and always the loss of a birth parent is devastating to a child, regardless of the reason they have been in care. The bond between a child and his/her birth parents is a powerful one. We have to understand this bonding and the loss experienced so we can get in touch with the child and work for a successful outcome.

During my first placement at the age of 16, the bond between my brother and me caused the disruption in my planned adoption. I am not sorry for the disruption today, as my brother and I were able to renew our relationship when I aged out of foster care. Until his death, we were able to have close regular contact. He was my best friend. He and his wife became foster parents to teenage boys for years.

Another example of the powerful bond is the placement of a 16-year old mother and her newborn baby in our home. In her short life, she had experienced a miscarriage, an abortion and then a normal beautiful baby boy. She had a very abusive past. Her mother's boyfriend had abused and raped her and was sent to prison for his crimes. She had then been placed with a relative who also abused her. She was removed and placed in foster care. They stayed in our home until she was 18 and graduated from high school. She had the opportunity to go to college or vocational school, but on graduation night, she called her mom and stepfather. After he had been released from prison, mom had married him, and the girl asked them to come get her and the baby. That evening, she went back to where she had vowed she would never go and took her baby with her.

We've heard the expression, "blood is thicker than water." Well, it certainly applies with most foster children. There is a strong bond in almost all cases. The burden is on the workers and foster parents to work with the birth parents to correct those things that created the foster care situation in the first place. This gives the child an opportunity to go home to a brighter and safer future.

A teenage girl and her baby were placed with me three different times for the same reason. Each time, mom had a different boyfriend who had sexually abused the girl. She had repeatedly told me that when she turned 18, her mom would be waiting outside our house for her and her baby to go back home. At the stroke of midnight, that is exactly what happened. She left our home, returning home to mom and the same guy that had abused her.

In this particular case, I've always hoped that something I did helped this young lady and made a difference in her adult life after she returned home.

Even though situations such as I just described happen, we have to understand that strong bond with the birth family. We have the task of working for the child's best interest as we try to maintain positive connections with their family. It's harmful for a child to hear negative attitudes about their parents coming from the foster parent.

While brushing the hair of a young child as she was talking about her mom, I was having a difficult time finding something good to say about her parent. Finally, I said that her mom had beautiful hair. That seemed to make her happy, and it kept me out of trouble.

It's very important that foster parents be nonjudgmental. Always try to send a positive message to the child, whenever possible, concerning their parents. This helps children feel good about themselves. Children often view their new caretakers as the enemy and blame the foster parent for the separation. Many times, they do not place any of the blame on the birth parent.

Birth parents often find it difficult to be friendly to foster parents until they realize that foster parents aren't a threat to them. Just like my story of chicken and dumplings, when the mom realized that I was not a threat to her, she offered thanks to me for helping her child. We have to work toward getting birth parents to realize that we aren't a threat before we can begin building trust. We have to realize that there are situations and times that birth parents are not able to work through their problems. This places a huge burden on the foster parent, but we must do everything we can for the child's sake.

Foster parents do not have an easy job. Often I'm sure you've wished as I have that the birth families would just go away. But they don't. We have to work together in the best interest of the child. We have to follow the rules and guidelines of the agency. We must work with birth parents who may be difficult, insensitive and inconsiderate. It's just not an easy job. But remember, the birth parents' ongoing involvement is a key element for successful foster care. The foster parents can do a number of things to positively increase parental involvement and help build good relationships.

In working with birth parents and focusing on the family as a whole unit, the reunification process becomes clearer. Foster parents must understand how birth parents feel about the removal of their child—their feelings of anger, frustration and resentment toward foster parents who are replacing them.

We are all a part of a team working together to reunite the family. Members of the team comprise the birth parents, the caretakers or foster parents, the worker and the child. We can not eliminate any part of this team and expect a successful return home. Once we're able to work together, then we open the door for birth parents to appreciate the care provided for their children.

For every child placed in your home, take his/her case and consider it individually. No one can give you a perfect pattern to follow to apply to every birth parent situation you encounter. Just do the best you can, and remember that a lot of responsibility is on your shoulders. You are being watched, whether you realize it or not. You are making an impression on that child in your home. Work closely with your worker and follow the information given to you to make decisions that are in best interest of your foster child. When your child is able to return home, your efforts will give you a feeling of success. You will know that you did your best.

Discipline and Foster Children

Why should I discipline a foster child any differently than I did my own children? This is the question often heard from foster parents as they are told corporal punishment must not be used. Well, it worked for my own children, so why should it be any different with my foster child?

Training on discipline and the foster child is required in my state. Parents must understand that the foster child's life has been very traumatic before they came into the system. In most cases, they have been through such abuse and misuse that different methods must be used that will teach rather than punish. You need to deal with the child's challenging behaviors in such a way that it teaches a better way instead of using inappropriate punishment.

The meaning of discipline is to teach. Children coming into custody need to be learn that there are better, safer and more protected ways to handle problems than some of the forms of punishment that have been used on them in the past.

In parenting children who have been neglected, abused or abandoned, foster parents will find that discipline is one of the hardest things they will encounter. We may get frustrated and upset while parenting the child in our care. Discipline should tell the child that they're valuable and important even when their behavior is not appropriate.

There is no secret method I can give you to be successful with regard to discipline. Each child is different and reacts differently to the discipline used. It takes training and a thorough understanding of each individual child's problem. What works for one may not work for another. However, the end result should always be the same. The consequence has to be appropriate for the behavior. Children should know that the discipline was administered out of love for them. They need to feel safe with their foster parents.

One of our foster daughters was a beautiful little red head, and you know what they say about the temper of red heads. She lived up to that cliché. She had a horrible, quick temper and was always trying my patience. I think sometimes she lay awake at night thinking about how she could aggravate the situation. She was a very difficult girl to handle at times, but hopefully I made some impression on her during the long term placement that we had with her.

She called me one day after her first son was born and said, "Mom, I used to think you were most horrible person and so mean to me. You made me mind and follow the rules of the house. Now that I have a son, I truly understand why you did what you did. I am having some of the same problems with him. He has such a temper, and I am forever having to punish him. Thank you so much for helping me and having patience with me. I know I tried your patience many times."

This is what it's all about for foster parents. It didn't happen very often that I got a thank you for my discipline, and I would not advise you to expect it either. I can't count the times I have been told by a child, "You aren't my mother, and I don't have to mind you." Oh, yes, as long as they are in my home, there's no question about that. I will administer discipline for wrong doing. As long as a child is doing something that is inappropriate, you are in control. You can never let the child see you back down from that or you will lose all control.

When giving rules, be sure that the child has a clear understanding of those rules. For example, when I told children to clean up their room, they would. But much to my surprise, their idea of cleaning was to kick everything under the bed and pile everything on top of the garbage can. I learned to be explicit and say things like, "Pick up all your clothes on the floor and put them in the dirty clothes hamper and empty the garbage can outside." We must be very specific in our instructions.

We need to keep in mind that these children have been through such traumatic experiences and have used certain survival behaviors before coming into care that are very hard to deal with at times. These behaviors may include lying, stealing, anger, depression, hoarding and inappropriate sexual behavior. Any one of these is reason for concern for foster parents. It is difficult to know how to reach the child while dealing with stressful behavior.

Perhaps one of the best methods is to ignore the behavior, especially if the child is acting out to get your attention. That is not to say that you don't keep a close watch on the behavior, but there are times that the behavior will stop if you just act as though you are not interested.

Listening to the child and asking questions as to why the particular behavior occurred can also help stop the behavior. Allowing the child to have a part in discussing what the outcome can help, as well. Give the child an opportunity to talk about what the options include. Often children are harder on themselves when they have the opportunity to make a decision. Drawing up a contract with an older child to explain what the consequences will be the next time rules are broken has been very effective in many cases. But it is imperative that the foster parents carry through with the consequence or all is in vain.

Choose carefully the time to deal with the behavior. During heated conflicts is not a good time. Have a cooling off period and then deal with it.

While having a very heated discussion with a 15-year-old, I said to the child, "Hold on, I'll be right back." I went into the yard and walked around for a period of time. When I came back inside, he asked where I had gone. "I put myself in time out to cool off." We wound up laughing about it, and I was able to handle the situation in a much cooler climate.

Foster children, particularly older ones, often learn quickly just the right buttons to push to set you off. Make certain that you understand this and don't let any situation get to that point. Once a child feels they know how to make you react, you're in trouble.

When you feel that the response to a child's request should be "No," it's okay to tell the child, "No." Make sure that you give a reason for saying it. I still remember my mom telling me, "No," on many occasions. When I asked why, her response was, "Because I said so." That's not a good answer. We need to be able to give a reason. Then allow your child to discuss your reason with you. There's always the possibility that we may be shown why we should change our answer to a "Yes."

One of the most effective tools used in my home to cut down on rebellion, including refusal to do a chore, homework or some other important task, was to offer a reward at end of a completed task. If I wanted a child to take out the garbage, I offered television time upon completion. There are any number of rewards that can be given for complying with duties or responsibilities.

Family meetings are also important, especially where children are having problems getting along with each other. Instead of having to deal with the problem individually, plan a family meeting where each child is given an opportunity without interruption to speak. They can bring out their concerns, problems, and anything else that is disturbing to them. This gives each child time to vent, to express concerns about other family members and has proved to be very effective and important in my home.

From time to time, inject humor into discipline. We can get too serious and damage our relationship with the child. Surprise your foster child and use your sense of humor when you can to stress a point. You will make an impression as you are teaching and stressing that a rule be followed.

My eight-year-old was having trouble on the school bus on year. I told him that I would be at school the next day to ride the bus home with him. I said that I'd sit beside him on the bus, and we'd see if I could behave like the bus driver wanted him to.

"You're joking, aren't you? Surely you wouldn't do that?" he said.

I let him stew about that for a while and then told him jokingly that we'd see how he did for the next few days and then we'd see about my ride. He took me at my word, and he didn't get another bad report that year.

Before you exercise any type of discipline, make certain that it fits the behavior, and addresses the problem in an appropriate method. If you do this, you can help your foster child learn a more suitable way to conduct themselves. Remember, you are using the discipline to help meet the needs of the child. Through your actions they will learn to problem solve appropriately, work through their problems positively and have a positive self-concept.

Using correct disciplinary techniques with a child is a great learning experience for foster parents and may be perfected over and over with each child that comes into the home.

Fostering Children and Sexual Abuse Issues

When a six-year-old little girl was placed in our home, we were told it was due to neglect by her mom and boyfriend. It was not long before I began to see the red flags that foster parents are taught to look for—the depression, the bedwetting, expressing too much knowledge about sex for a child her age, her actions around other males and also how she played with her dolls.

After a discussion with the agency worker, we made an appointment to see a therapist trained in child sexual abuse. Our little foster daughter denied that anyone had ever touched her inappropriately. It was not long after the first two counseling visits that she and I were in the grocery store when she saw a member of her family. She immediately began to shake and cry. She climbed under the grocery buggy, drawing up into the fetal position. I suddenly knew the answer to the questions that had been bothering me since she came into our home. From her actions, this had to be the perpetrator.

Foster parents need to be educated, to acquire skills and compassion in order to adequately address issues of sexual abuse with the children who are place in their homes. Foster parents should ask the agency worker placing the child if the child has been sexually abused and if they are sexually active. Understanding this on the front end will help to be able to more effectively deal with the problem. You need to become desensitized to the subject of sexual abuse so that you can discuss issues with the child without appearing shocked, hesitant or embarrassed.

Rules governing how the family handles private issues in the home, such as dress, bathroom and respect for personal space needs to be discussed with the child upon placement. One of the best ways to accomplish this is to have a family meeting. These meetings may be held regularly or on a per need basis with the opportunity for everyone to express their thoughts and feelings about certain issues that may be or could create disturbances. This is an excellent opportunity to lay out all of the family's rules. Allow time for questions from each family member. Make it clear how children should report any uncomfortable situations that might arise within the home.

Any child can be a victim of sexual abuse, and abusers are seldom "dirty old men." It can be a family member, a trusted friend, a teacher or the person whom you would least expect to be an abuser. Sexual abuse is never forgotten by the survivor, and often it's kept hidden through fear, threats and manipulation.

We worked with a sexually abused boy who came into our home, and it took a long time to get him to disclose his sexual abuse. His abuser had told the child that if he ever told anyone his sister would be his next victim. Having a younger sister still in the birth home, the child was petrified and traumatized by this threat.

The child must be made to understand that the sexual abuse was not his/her fault. It is very important for them to understand that foster parents are there to believe, support and listen to anything they want to disclose. Relate to the child that they are safe, that you want to help, that you will believe their story and take whatever steps are needed to make certain that it won't ever happen again. Letting the child know that you won't judge them is very important in getting them to disclose to you what they have been through.

When the child tells you what happened, it is very important that you let the child talk. Don't probe for more information or promise that you won't tell anyone. It is most important that you do not respond with horror or show any expression other than compassion as you listen. Let the child know that you will not share this information with anyone except the agency worker.

If children's issues with regard to sexual abuse are not addressed, the long-term effects can be horrifying. Substance abuse, prostitution, running away, eating disorders, suicide, unwanted pregnancy or even becoming an abuser of other children are possible outcomes.

Caring for the sexually abused child may be different from caring for other children. Each case is different, and additional steps may be necessary to reach the child. Counseling is extremely important in helping to rebuild trust in the child. If the therapist allows it, foster parents should attend the meetings. It is so important that the child know that you are interested and involved, that you want to help them overcome this tragedy in their lives.

A sexually abused child coming into the foster home will not come in to the home eager to talk, nor will that child immediately show trust in their new caretakers. Sometimes it takes months and in some cases, years before we can gain insight into their troubled minds and establish the trust required for them to relate their abuse.

When Mary was placed in our home, I was told that she had probably been sexually active. There were two teenage girls there at the time, and we had an opportunity to go to a weekend retreat. Teens were paired up for room accommodations with chaperones in rooms nearby.

During the early morning hours, I was awakened by the younger girl who stated that Mary had slipped out earlier. Along with another foster parent chaperone, we began our search and found Mary in a room with two teenage boys. We didn't have to guess what had happened and immediately took steps to bring Mary back to my room for the duration of the night. I resolved to deal with the behavior the next morning. Through that experience, I learned a tremendous lesson. From then on, I stayed in the room with girls I knew to be sexually active when there were males nearby.

The vocabulary of a child who has been a victim of sexual abuse may be filled with words that we don't normally use in our homes. As embarrassing as it may be for us, we need to handle this problem in such a way that the child does not feel shame or guilt. We cannot let the child feel threatened either. These are words the child has learned and used in his/her former environment. We must work carefully and consistently with the child toward more appropriate forms of communication.

Foster parents must be aware of the symptoms of sexual abuse in a foster child.

They include:

- The way in which a girl plays with her dolls
- Physical injury to the genitals and/or anal area
- Repeated urinary tract infections
- Bedwetting
- Unusual fear of being touched
- Excessive masturbation
- Emotional reactions of fear to bath time, bedtime or other new experience.

Older children may exhibit behaviors such as flaunting nudity, being sexually active, and displaying very seductive behavior. All of these known red flags can indicate sexual abuse.

From my experience, when dealing with children who have been sexually abused, it is important to be patient, to listen to the child and to observe their actions. You must set firm but caring limits on any inappropriate behavior. You must be comfortable with sex education so that you can discuss issues with the child as they arise. Keep a log of the child's progress for your own knowledge and for sharing with the worker. Sex abuse training is very helpful for foster parents. In these classes, you can learn why sexual abuse occurs and how to care for the child who has been sexually abused.

Your attitude and assistance to the child and his/her family is crucial when preparing the child for a return home. Try to be a role model for the birth family and present yourself as a supportive unit in time of need. The child's future may depend on the action and support of the foster family.

Saving Discouraged Foster Parents

Foster parents often become discouraged and experience disappointments in various areas with the child placed in their home. How many, many times I've had foster parents tell me that they are so tired of rules changing, workers changing, having to work with irate birth parents, not receiving all the information needed on the child, not enough financial support, and so many other things. I, too, have felt many of these concerns and disappointments.

When you've been fostering for a while, it's only normal that one morning you get up and things just aren't working the way you'd like. You seem to be getting more and more discouraged, and things that didn't bother you before now take on added significance. You begin to think that you can't take it any more. When this happens, it's time to take a step back. It's helpful to remember the reasons you became a foster parent. Think about the role you play in the lives of your foster children and the responsibility you have to them. Diligently examine those reasons that got you into your fostering experience. Has anything changed?

The advice I often give is that when you are feeling overwhelmed, stressed, and ready to just quit, do a self evaluation. Remind yourself about the children you have helped. Work to rebuild your healthy sense of self-esteem. Know that you are important to yourself, to your family and to each of your foster children.

At one time or another, you may feel burnt out. The definition of burnout, according to the Merriam Webster's Collegiate Dictionary, is "exhaustion of physical or emotional strength or motivation usually as a result of prolonged stress or frustration." Burnout can creep upon us insidiously. One day, you may wake up and find that you don't want to foster anymore. There is no longer any joy or excitement for you, no anticipation. Extended periods of feeling burnt out can lead to a negative attitude towards work and life. Feelings of frustration and anger can intensify.

Do you ever have to deal with anger? Not a child's anger, but your own? I have many times. It's hard sometimes for me to hold back my anger. Most people feel intense anger at times. Through anger, we express the way we feel. But anger must be released in the right way. Otherwise, you'll be like a pot of boiling water with the lid left on. If the steam doesn't escape, the water will finally boil over and blow its top. When that happens, it's no fun for anyone, and you can destroy a relationship that you've been trying to build.

Anger can be a good thing at times. When kids are treated unfairly, we can sometimes teach that anger can help them stand up for themselves. The hard part is learning what to do with these strong feelings and when to do it. It's important to not let anger make you lose control.

Don't let repeated anger be your reason for becoming discouraged and creating the feeling that you want to quit fostering. Determine what situation is causing you to become angry, search for a solution and then work to resolve the problem. Once you find a solution, your anger and discouraged feelings will dissipate.

Throughout the time I've been a foster parent, I've wanted to quit at least once each year. I think I've had a lot of the good reasons for becoming discouraged, but there's one thing that keeps me coming back to my life's calling. It always comes back to the children and doing what I can do in their best interest. I also remember when I was in foster care. I remember the trauma, the loneliness, the hurt, the lack of love and the lack of a family. No child should have to go through periods of their life feeling as I did. Foster care is not always easy for the parent or the child.

One of the most discouraging times for foster parents is when they have been faced with an allegation. Many foster parents have quit after an unfounded allegation because of the trauma they experienced while awaiting the outcome. In our country, a person is supposed to be considered innocent until proven guilty, but with foster parents it seems like we are guilty until proven innocent.

Foster parents are often asked to take children that they feel that they are not equipped to handle, or they allow themselves to become overloaded with too many children in the home. With a very problematic child, I could get overloaded very easily with just one more child in my home. We need to be careful not to overload ourselves. Do not take children that you know you cannot handle. If you do, you may throw in the towel and quit, and we cannot afford to lose any caring foster family.

One of my most terrifying moments came when a young boy was placed in my home. It was his first placement. The worker was not certain, but felt that there had been some sexual abuse somewhere within his past. One evening, he completely lost control and was threatening to harm me or anyone else that got in his way. He was in a vicious rage and had to even be held back from grabbing the butcher knife. He made me a believer that there were some children I could not handle.

As I waited for the crisis team to arrive at 1:30 a.m., the child had begun to calm down somewhat, but I was feeling more than ready to throw in the towel, to end this fostering escapade. Sitting at my computer, I thought about how and when to break the news to my worker. But then I began remembering my days of uncertainty when I was in foster care. I remember the feelings of uncertainty about my future. Then I thought about what could have made this young child spin so far out of control.

It had begun when he had been told that his visit with his mom was not going to be possible the next weekend. He had become very angry and upset, stating that he wanted to go home to his mother and didn't want to be in a foster home. I had merely said that I hoped things could be worked out and that he would get to go home to his mother soon. Immediately, he began to show such extreme anger as he screamed at me, "Don't talk about my mother! Don't even mention my mother!" This was the beginning of the horrific two-hour experience.

After I checked on him when the crisis team left, I began to re-evaluate his problems, thinking about all of the things he might have gone through. Once again, I put my priorities in order and sat down and wrote these words:

A Little Girl's Letter to Her Foster Parents

Foster mom and dad, please don't give up on me,
My problems and needs, I know you can see,
I still don't understand why I was suddenly moved and placed,
In a strange home, it's something no one should have to face.
But you opened your heart, shared your home and your life,
You know mine was so filled with such trouble and strife.
You helped me and made me so proud to be your foster kid,
If only here for a while, I know God saw everything you did.
Did I do something to make you want to give up and quit?
I thought we were family, now why do we have to split?
I've asked God to show me how to help you change your mind,
I hope it's not my fault or that I've ever been unkind.
Maybe tomorrow you'll see it differently, continue, and remain
Please don't quit, let me stay with you, I have yet so much to gain.
You are important to me, and other foster kids they need you too,
Tonight, I'll ask God to tell you that you can't be through.

Anyone can get burnt out. There's nothing wrong with taking time to rest from all the strain and stress that comes with the foster care system. Foster parents are needed, and I'm certain your agency would prefer that you take time off from fostering for a short period of time than to lose you. Check out your options if you feel you must take some time of respite.

There was a time that foster parents were not given the opportunity to attend meetings of any kind, including court hearings or foster care review board meetings. We were not allowed to know anything about the child except the first name and the small amount of board payment that we would receive. Those days have changed. We now have an obligation to get involved, to attend meetings. The more information we have, the more we can help to find permanency for the child. We need to know what the child has gone through and to understand their problems. Understanding helps many foster parents deal with whatever issues may arise and keeps them from throwing in that proverbial towel.

Another outlet when you become discouraged can be exercise. Exercising helps you to relax and relieve you of stress and anxiety. You don't have to spend a lot of time exercising, just enough to help you gain a little added strength that will enable you to deal with everyday problems. We need regular daily exercise of some kind for our health, if for no other reason. I don't always get to follow my own advice, but it helps to spend time alone relaxing. Get a sitter, go to an event or do something just for you. Foster couples, go out to a quiet dinner. The kids will still be there, along with the problems, when you return. If you take time for each other, you will be better able to handle whatever comes your way.

Getting together with other foster parents to share stories and concerns is also important. This helps us understand that we aren't alone. When we see others sharing our concerns, we gain courage and strength to try it a little longer. We need the support of one another.

When you have a concern or become discouraged or upset over something pertaining to foster care, take it to a higher level. Call the worker, the supervisor, a legislator or a judge. Take your concerns to the right person. Don't throw up your hands and quit. Talk about the problem and get it out of your system.

Throughout my years fostering, I've kept mostly teens. Whenever I've felt discouraged and disgusted at something that one of them had done, I often thought, just as soon as they leave my home, I'm closing it. But I discovered that if I addressed the problem with the child, a solution could be found. Communication is a great way to keep from becoming discouraged.

Finally, I would suggest counseling. Attending counseling sessions with the child in your home can often help to open doors of communication that will enable you to understand what your child is experiencing.

Foster parents can and do make a difference. Children in care need good quality homes, and we need all of those caring parents who have the courage to share their hearts and homes! As stated in Proverbs 31:8, we should, "Speak up for those who cannot speak for themselves, for the rights of all who are destitute."

Fostering Has Its Rewards

When people consider becoming foster parents, inevitably they wonder how they will be able to handle all the problems and baggage that a child can bring with them. "How are we going to let the child stay in our home for a while and then be taken from us? Will we be able to handle it? What rewards and benefits come with foster parenting?" So many questions cause concern when making such an important decision.

This is a normal reaction, but training and preparation in the area of foster care is readily available. State agencies have ably planned pre-service training that introduces prospective foster parents to the ins and outs of the child welfare system. Through this training, an understanding of what is required of the parents, what is necessary for the child and how to go about becoming foster parents is gained.

Even before training begins, prospective parents must have genuine concern and love for children and a desire to help create a better life for a child who has been abused, neglected or abandoned. Sharing their love and their home is one of the greatest rewards that a foster parent can receive for the work that they do. Reaching out to a child in need is a noble act and its own reward.

One of the most memorable placements who came to our home was a teenage boy who had been left at the county jail by his father who said, "Do what you want to with him because I will not take him back home with me."

My heart went out to this young man, who was so broken up and hurting. Immediately, we offered to give him a home, and he was with us until he aged out of the system. On his 18th birthday, we asked Bill, "What do you want for your birthday?"

Our hearts swelled with pride when he responded, "Will you help me change my last name to yours?" With humbled hearts, we saw to it that his wish was granted.

In recent years, great strides have been made to involve foster parents in decisions that affect the life of their foster child. Foster parents are now recognized by state agencies as playing an important part in the life and future of the child in their home. Foster parents are more involved than ever in the child's life during placement. They are invited to attend meetings with the birth family, attend permanency plan sessions and attend court hearings. Who else besides the foster parent, who has the child full time, could share information on the child that is beneficial to the judge and the other professional people making decisions surrounding the future of the child in care?

These changes have helped foster parent in so many ways. They now get to meet the birth parents, which allows them to analyze and understand the problems that led to the removal from the home. Foster parents are able to see positive changes through these meetings over time, which can greatly influence finding permanency for the child. It is so rewarding to know that you've had a part in helping a child return to parents that have made changes or improvements that will be of benefit to the child. When a foster parent sees happiness on the face of the child in care because he can now return to a home that has a more positive environment than the one he left, all of the hard work seems so worthwhile. Foster parents gain incredible feelings of accomplishment from these moments.

A special moment in my fostering life was a 10-year-old boy who had been placed in my home. He had a great amount of anger and hostility toward being in foster care. It took time and a lot of work to convince him that I was not replacing his mom, that I wanted only to work with him until Mom could get things straightened out. It was not accomplished overnight, but in the final days as he prepared to go home, I felt proud of the fact that the anger toward me had vanished. I will always remember and cherish that big hug and smile he gave me on the day he went home.

A majority of children who are placed in care have not had a home environment conducive to a productive adulthood. There are many older children who age out of the system and do not return to their birth home for various reasons. Foster parents of these children are regarded as surrogate parents who continue to be a resource for help and encouragement with a room always available for vacations and special occasions.

I have kept contact with many of the older children I have had in my home after they left to go to college. Some return to visit on vacation days and holidays. On one occasion, my foster child invited the birth parent to visit in our home for a holiday.

It is such a joy when a former foster child, who is now a mother, calls and I hear a little voice say, "Grandmother, can we come over to visit with you today?" What a great blessing to have a fostering experience such as this! Foster parents often do not realize the lasting impressions they make on the child while he/she is in their home.

Fostering is not for those looking to adopt. Fostering is temporary, but the majority of adoptions in almost every state are by foster parents. This is truly one of the greatest rewards of fostering—helping a child find permanency. Once the child's rights have been terminated and the child has been in the foster home for a period of time, adoption can become a possibility. Many foster parents take that final step toward giving the child love, permanency and a future in the home where he/she has already become part of a family.

My thoughts as a foster parent were certainly not to become an adoptive parent in the beginning. I was not interested in adoption. I had three birth children and a stepson, but when the time came and rights were terminated, adoption became reality. Twice, we were faced with the decision, and each boy had been in our home for a long period of time. The response to the worker was simply, "Yes, we will adopt. They have a home permanently with us." I know that many foster parents have felt the same way when the opportunity to give a permanent loving home to their child was presented to them.

One of the happiest moments for one young foster couple with whom I worked was the day that a baby was placed in their home. The worker had indicated that there was a great possibility that rights would be terminated. This couple had not been able to have a child of their own and had decided to foster. When this baby was placed into their home and they were told that rights are to be terminated, the worker had already found his permanent loving home. So many foster parents who have adopted have felt the happiness that this couple is about to experience.

As a former foster child who had experience in foster care as a teen, I appreciate the opportunity to have shared in the lives of so many children. I know that almost every foster parent would agree with me that though every experience is not always positive, there's not much in life that can offer such gratifying rewards.

A few days ago, I was in a shopping mall, and I was greeted by a very nice looking, well-mannered young man who I did not immediately recognize. "Miss Betty, how are you doing?" he said. Taken by surprise, it took me a moment to realize who he was. We talked for a few moments. He told where he was living, where he was working and that he was home for a visit. I left him feeling very emotional and holding back the tears as I remembered what he said to me, "Miss Betty, I want to thank you for helping me. I'll never forget you."

To me, this is what fostering is all about—knowing that we make a difference in someone's life.

Yes, being a foster parent definitely has its rewards.

My Personal Letter
to Foster Parents

Fostering can be so rewarding, and at the same time, discouraging, stressful and traumatic. My life as a foster parent has been filled with many up and downs, but I can promise you that it has never been boring or unexciting. My days have always been filled with unexpected and unanticipated events. My best advice to new foster parents would be to always add laughter and fun to your fostering life.

At times, we may come at a point when we need a shoulder to cry on, when we need support and understanding for the things we face in our every day life. Agency workers have been trained to be there for us, but foster parents need more than that. We need the support of one another.
I have personally been there. I've felt like I had no one to turn to. For that reason, I have been compelled to reach out touch the lives of others who have devoted themselves to children in care. It always helped me to talk to a person with experience, a person who bore the scars that sometimes come with fostering.

Discouragement is something that a lot of foster parents feel occasionally. I felt that same discouragement strongly one evening as I reflected on how my day had not turned out as I had anticipated it would. I know that so many foster parents can relate to those feelings.

A Normal Day

I awoke this morning excited to have a day all to myself
I think I'll check out the library and the new bookshelf
The foster kids are all off to school
Time to relax
Peace and quiet for me
I'll enjoy it to the max.

Wait…is that the phone that I hear?
Guess I should pick up
Could be the school
Or maybe Mary wants to gossip
The placement worker wants me to take a child
She says he's no problem
A good kid, just a little wild
Guess I'll give it a try
That's what foster parents usually do
After this one, I'll tell you again I am through.

Pick the child up
Gather some clothes for him to wear
Register him in school, get physical check
Too much to do
Already feeling despair
My day is not going as planned
What happened to my serenity?
My new child tells me he's been busted for drugs
When are we going to learn to say no?
But we can help a child
Surely, it will be worth it, though.

Not many peaceful days for foster parents to claim
Putting a smile on the face of a child

That's the name of the game
Guess I'll just forget about having quiet time today
School bus time
Kids will want a snack right away
I'll just carry on as I have for so many long years
It's my way of life
I shouldn't complain
Or express my fears
God in heaven must have a special place
For foster parents like me and you
There are days I feel I'm about ready
How about you?

How many times has a foster parent's day turned out just like mine? I'm sure a lot of you can relate to days just like this. Sharing laughter and taking time out to enjoy what we're doing is so important. I like to relate in my speeches some of the incidents that have brought tears and laughter over the years.

A young girl came to us at the age of seven. Susie was a lovely little girl, but often a headache for one of our foster teenage sons. Our county did not have an emergency shelter, and our home was used often for this purpose. Children were in and out for short periods of time regularly. Susie was constantly complaining to me that Bill, our teenage son, was always giving other kids a nickname and she couldn't understand why he never gave her one.

One afternoon, she came running up to me very excited, and said, "Mom, Mom, Guess what! Bill gave me a nickname." She seemed so proud, and I asked her what it was. "He called me, Hemorrhoid...Mom what does that mean?"

I tried to tell her in the kindest way possible. "Honey, that means a pain in the butt." To soothe her feelings, I reminded her that Bill did give her a nickname. As foster parents, we have to be prepared for those special moments and to make the best of any situation, regardless of what it is.

Foster parents have to be prepared for anything that we might encounter, but we're never truly prepared for some of the bizarre things that we go through. One of my most unexpected experiences was to have a live torpedo found 100 feet from my backyard.

We had a set of 15-year-old twins, both seven feet tall, and although they were often a joy to have around, they lived at times in a fantasy world. I was sweeping off the carport one afternoon, and the boys had been out in the woods wandering around, when they came running toward me out of breath. "Miss Betty, Miss Betty, call the police, Call the police."

I told them to calm down and asked, "What is the problem?"

They both squealed out at the same time," We found a torpedo back there!"

We live in a rural area with no water around except a small pond next door. Knowing the boys as I did, I said, "Let's wait until Pop gets home. I'll let him call the police." When my husband came in, they were still excited and ran up to him, "Pop, you've got to go with us to see that torpedo and call the police. It's sticking up in the ground, but we kicked and kicked it until we got it loose. We've seen pictures of something like this in our books at school. It was a torpedo! We got scared and dropped it."

Charles told them to let him rest for a moment and then he'd go with them. He told me he knew he wouldn't get any rest so he'd better go see what it was that they had found.

I knew from the look on Charles' face he had found something frightening. He called the sheriff's department and told them there was a torpedo in the field. Charles could hear the deputies laughing across the room, amused that some 'nut foster parent' had found a torpedo in his back field.

When the investigator came in and heard who had called, he said he knew Charles Hastings, and if Charles said there was a torpedo in his field his deputy had better get out there and see.

The deputy came back from the field white as a sheet and immediately called for help. Within minutes there were ambulances, fire trucks, FINA, sheriff cars and by midnight an Army bomb squad was on the scene.

I often wonder what our neighbors thought about all the excitement, lights, sirens and confusion. I'm sure they thought that someone had been murdered.

The Army sergeant said he wanted talk with the boys who had found the torpedo. He wanted to alert them that they had done a very dangerous thing by kicking and picking up such a hazardous material. Charles wondered aloud about what the chances were of having a torpedo fall into our back yard ever again? The sergeant ordered us to keep the incident quiet.

Do you think two 15-year-old boys were quiet? No. One of them had snuck down and took a picture of the torpedo. There was a picture and article in the local newspaper the next week.

We still don't know where the torpedo came from. The investigation determined that it was a torpedo used in training exercises and possibly dropped from a helicopter transporting it from the Army base to the Navel base. We never heard anything else from anyone. After that, I learned to always expect the unexpected. Life in fostering is filled with unusual events that will never cease to amaze you.

I hope that the topics I have addressed in this book will be of some benefit to you as you continue helping our children in care. Personally, I feel my life's mission has been to serve the best interest of children, promote foster care wherever I go and to support, encourage and help to educate foster parents as they care for children in custody.

Nothing touches me more and explains the reason I do what I do more than the following scriptures.

"For I was hungry and ye gave me meat; I was thirsty, and ye gave me drink, I was a stranger, and ye took me in.

When saw we thee a stranger and took thee in, naked and clothed thee?

Inasmuch as ye have done it unto one of the least of these, my brethren, ye have done it unto me."

Matt 25: 35-36, 38, 40

Author's Note

I want to thank God for His divine help throughout my life. It was through His goodness that I came to understand the reasons for the valleys I encountered and the mountaintops I experienced. I am humbled by the power of His saving grace in my life. I hope I've learned throughout my many experiences to be considerate, sympathetic and thoughtful of others, especially the dedicated foster parents who do God's work.

A very special thank you belongs to Brian Arnold of Kimberling City, Missouri, who is an evangelist, one-handed piano player, gospel singer and songwriter. He is not only my prayer partner and a good friend, but he is the one God used to help teach me to appreciate His divine blessings in my every day life. It's been my privilege to work with Brian and his The King's Table Ministry. Brian's inspiration, encouragement and insistence motivated me to write this book.

I owe a special appreciation to Mike Kinnamon of Music Central Management in Nashville, Tennessee, who has been so inspirational and understanding of the dream I had to write and publish this book. It was through Mike that I was introduced to the very talented, understanding and patient author and editor, Susan D. Mustafa. She took my writing and polished it into the finished copy. I do not feel it was by accident that this wonderful, gifted person was sent to be of assistance to me from the very city where I was placed during my years in foster care, Baton Rouge, Louisiana.

Thank you also to Walt Mayeux of Graphics, Etc. in Prairieville, Louisiana, whose talent created the cover of this book.

For each foster parent whose path I have crossed through the years, it's been a joy and a pleasure. I've been given so many opportunities to share training, experiences and laughter that I hope helped lighten the load of what they encountered daily in their fostering lives. I appreciate each comment, each written note and each word of encouragement that helped me deal with each tomorrow. I use these experiences now to encourage and help others.

I owe so much to my birth children—my son, Edward Daigle, and my daughters, Tamela White and LeAnn Dunlap. Thank you for having patience with Mom's frequent travels and for your help and understanding as you've generously shared me with so many others through the years. I love you dearly.

For every child who has passed through my home, it's been my pleasure to know you. Even though there were heartaches at time, I hope that you left with a ray of light shining through your spirit and the feeling that you gained something positive during your stay in the Hastings home.

Every foster parent shares an understanding about what is expected of them, as well as the ultimate goals for the children placed in their care. Through laughter and heartaches, we all work together and separately to make the lives of children a little brighter. I hope this book gives you helpful guidance and a better understanding of the issues you face as you continue to make such a difference in the life of a child.

May God bless and watch over each of you.

Accolades

I have known Betty Hastings for many years and have always admired her courage to take on challenges and help children in need. She has never hesitated to speak truth to power in Tennessee, always seeking the "right thing" be done for the children. While serving as commissioner of the Tennessee Department of Children's Services, Betty was a trusted advisor. She always spoke the truth, always represented the best interest of the children and never hesitated to disagree if I was not moving the department in the right direction. She helped reform a dysfunctional foster care system, ensuring that children had a voice in the governor's office. Since leaving Tennessee, I have traveled across the country evaluating various states' systems of care, always remembering the valuable lessons she taught me in Tennessee. She is a very special advocate who demands a fair, balanced and accountable system of care for children.

—George W. Hattaway, public policy consultant,
Child Welfare League of America

Betty Hastings has crisscrossed Tennessee a thousand times over in pursuit of ensuring that every person is aware that kids need good, strong families. Whether through advocating for needed legislation in support of foster parents, leading the Tennessee Foster and Adoptive Care Association or caring for children in her own home, Betty Hastings has been and continues to be a leading advocate for this country's most vulnerable children. This collection of Betty's wisdom and experience is a valuable read for any person who is considering and feeling a special call to serve as a foster parent.

—Elizabeth Black, executive director,
Office of Child Permanency, Department of Children's Services

Certainly anyone who has opened her home to care for 350 children over a period of 30 years has credibility as an "expert" on foster parenting and the public child welfare "system." And certainly such a person must have a huge heart motivated out of sense of ministry. Betty Hastings is such a person. She has seen the best and the worst of the foster care system, and in her professional career she has planted many seeds in the hearts of the children in her care and in the hearts of hundreds of foster parents and child welfare workers. She challenges all of us to live up to high standards of compassion and professional care. She knows we cannot provide effective care without being in connection with a broad support system—both for ourselves as caregivers and for our children. I am pleased to count Betty Hastings as a colleague and friend, and I am confident her book can help us all to become better caregivers for children in need.

—Art Masker, president/CEO,
Holston United Methodist Home for Children

Not many people can attest to the world of foster care like Betty Hastings can. Having herself been in foster care, she has the child perspective as well as the foster parent perspective after numerous years of bringing kids into her own home. Betty is also a gifted presenter and writer in the arena of foster care/adoption. She utilizes her insight and humor to teach and guide those who are on the same mission field. It is my privilege to have known this woman that I call "Mom" since we met through the National Foster Parent Association years ago. My family and I truly see her as a gift from God. I believe this book is too.

—M. Kim Combes, M.Ed, director,
Combes Counseling and Consultation

Few people know foster care and adoption from the inside out. Betty speaks the truth with wisdom and great compassion. She shares her story in a way that is not sensational, but rather gives voice to each child who has experienced foster care. Betty is an advocate, a trainer and an advisor. But most importantly, she is a foster and adoptive parent who has forever changed the lives of those with whom she has shared her heart.

Important to me, she is my dear friend and advisor. Knowing Betty has improved my practice in child welfare. I thank Betty for her guidance, friendship and great gift of this book.

—Michael McSurdy, past-director of Foster Care, State of Tennessee

My wife and I have been foster parents for over 35 years. Along the way we've met many other foster parents who have been an inspiration to us. Betty Hastings is one of those special persons from whom I've learned a lot as I've come to know her both as a friend and a source of knowledge and encouragement as a foster parent. She has hosted me in Tennessee and has been in our home in Minnesota. Our paths have crossed often as we both have a similar passion for kids, foster parenting, and improvement of the system that provides care to foster kids. I would describe her as a little bulldog with the roar of lion. If one is facing difficult issues, Betty is someone that you want on your side!

—Randy Ruth, past-president, National Foster Parent Association

Betty is a tireless individual who has spent her entire adult life advocating for the betterment of the child welfare system. Tennessee was the first state to draft a bill of rights for foster parents and Betty was right there, spearheading the effort for the state legislature to approve the bill. Since then, 12 additional states have used the Tennessee template and were successful in legislating a bill of rights. As long as I have known Betty, I have admired her gift as a trainer and speaker. She is always so poised and at ease, regardless of the audience.

—Karen Jorgenson, past NFPA executive director

As the editor of training for foster parents, Foster Care Support Network (FCSN), caring and knowledgeable people like Betty Hastings are extremely valuable for both myself, and more importantly, for the foster parents who read our monthly training.

Betty has shared some of the insights she's learned from decades of experience as a foster parent for our FCSN training. This has included both her willingness to be interviewed for articles I've written, and

writing she has undertaken herself, most recently, "Understanding, Treating Attachment Disorder" in January 2008.

The fact that Betty has provided keynotes for various foster parent conferences and workshops also speaks volumes about her knowledge of foster care. In this day and age, it is not that difficult to find general parenting advice online. But it is very difficult, if not impossible, to find information on the Internet that adequately addresses the unique topics involved in foster care—and from someone with her wealth of experience.

—Mike Jacquart, editor, Foster Care Support Network

Betty Hastings is a national treasure. She has made her life's work in the unselfish service of our nation's most vulnerable children and the surrogate families who open their hearts and homes to care for them. As an engaging speaker, her genuine, natural warmth comforts the audience through tough subject matter. Betty never forgets her humble beginnings as a foster child herself and with her gentle humor carries the reader through her own personal journey from orphan to foster parent to adoptive mother and finally a respected national child welfare advocate. Betty has changed the road for those who follow in her path. She has changed the face of foster care in America.

—Michalle Shown-Rodriguez, executive director,
Sierra Association of Foster Families, California

I have known Betty on a professional level for 10 years. She is an important part of the foster care system in our state. Her knowledge and expertise is very instrumental in ensuring the safety of our children through her countless hours of training to the Foster Parent Association. Betty is a strong support for families who have opened their homes to the abused and neglected. She devotes her time and effort in helping families understand the demands and rewards of foster parenting. Betty's book will be a lasting tribute to the community and families. It will also serve as a much needed resource of information and insight into foster care.

—Norma Wallace, foster parent support worker,
Department of Children's Services, State of Tennessee

Betty recreated herself by the amazing and extraordinary work she has done for children and foster parents from all walks of life. I have seen her laugh, I have seen her jump for joy, I have seen her stressed to no end, and I have seen her cry and yet, I have never seen her quit. Betty, as one foster parent and friend to another, I am so proud of you and I am convinced that only you could walk in these shoes to tell the told and untold stories of your journey.

—Joyce McDaniel-Lewis, vice president,
National Foster Parent Association

Betty is a woman who has gone through life in an extremely unselfish manner. She could have used her experiences growing up in the welfare system to demean and diminish the character of others. Certainly, the terrible experiences she faced could have been detrimental not only to her own character, but to family, social workers and others who were responsible for her dilemma. Instead, she chose to educate and train those who, like herself, give daily to the needs of foster and adoptive children. She remains, truly, one of my heroes. Through her strength, her belief in herself and her ability to create innovative and interesting presentations, Betty gives a realistic view to all who share in her passion, creating quality homes for the children.

—Sharon Carlson, executive director,
Georgia Foster Adoptive Parents Association

I have had the pleasure as well as the opportunity to work with Betty Hastings as a foster parent with The Tennessee Department of Children's Services over the last eight years. Several of those years with Betty were spent training foster parents in the areas of Foster Parent Bill of Rights and Fostering the Delinquent Youth. Her ability and passion regarding her role as a foster parent is amazing. Betty has demonstrated extraordinary skills and understanding of the importance being a foster parent.

—Servella Terry, Department of Children Services, State of Tennessee

Betty Hastings is a strong advocate for Tennessee's children. Her experiences as a former foster child and as a long time foster and adoptive parent give her a unique perspective in discussions regarding permanency for youth in out-of-home care. She has volunteered with the North American Council on Adoptable Children (NACAC) for 10 years, and has worked on the local, state, and national levels to further the cause of foster and adopted children. Betty has a wonderful sense of humor that serves her well in a very difficult field.

—Jeanette Wiedemeier Bower, project manager,
North American Council on Adoptable Children

About the Author

Betty Daigle Hastings has worked within the child welfare system for more than 30 years. As a teenager, she experienced life as a foster child, which influenced her decision to foster other children as an adult. To date, she has fostered more than 350 children and adopted two. She also has three children of her own.

Betty has been very active in the foster care system, serving as president of the Tennessee Foster Adoptive Care Association for six years. She has also served her state as the president of the Tennessee Foster Adoptive Association for six years. She has served on the National Foster Parent Association in various positions, including that of chairman of the state affiliates.

In her role as an inspirational speaker, she has shared her knowledge about foster care through keynote speeches at numerous association conferences across the country. Betty is the published author of many articles about foster care, and she conducts workshops and training seminars for foster/adoptive parents. She also works closely with Evangelist Brian Arnold and The King's Table Ministry in Tennessee.

Betty was instrumental in the adoption of the Foster Parent Bill of Rights law in Tennessee and subsequently worked with other states to create similar bills that used the Tennessee Law as their model.

She has also served as a member of the Tennessee Governor's Children Cabinet and as a member of the Tennessee Supreme Court Permanency Planning Commission.

Currently, Betty continues with her mission to promote the welfare of children in foster care throughout the United States through writing, teaching, speaking and sharing love and wisdom with foster parents and children in care.